Testimonials

This book is a testament to life, light, hope and love. That's easy to understand! So is the author, my wonderful friend, Janie Lidey! Get ready to be blessed.

~ Butch Baker ~
Senior Vice President of Creative Services, HoriPro
Entertainment in Nashville, Tennessee

Janie Lidey is a transformational leader and an outstanding role model. Through her many leaps of faith, she has proven that persistence and vision can lead to great success in one's chosen profession.

~ Carol Comeau ~
Retired Superintendent, Anchorage School District

Beyond the musical accolades and excellence Janie Lidey has cultivated in her life, her greatest strength is her almost magical ability to connect with people from every walk of life, inspiring them to believe in themselves and their ability to make a positive difference in the world.

~ Michael T. Graham ~
Chief Academic Officer, Anchorage School District

Passionate Enthusiasm + Positive Energy + Performance Excellence = Janie Lidey is Perfect!

~ MK Mueller ~
Author of *8 to Great: The Powerful Process for Positive Change*

Music is the universal language that will lift the world and make it sing in unison. I believe the message Janie Lidey brings in her stories and songs is what will fuel the movement!

~ Gene Bedley ~
National Educator of the Year and Impact Coordinator for Lift Up America.

One of the most talented singer songwriters that has exceeded my expectations in the global media markets.

~ Danie Cortese ~
International Music Publicist at DCE International

Janie's first book was a shiny rock, but this one is a diamond! Her stories, songs and sincere message are interwoven beautifully!

~ Dorena Montgomery ~
Longtime Friend

Janie's voice and music are like a prayer. They simply heal.

~ Cedric Sanders ~
Actor, Singer

Leap of Faith

For Joeie, 😊

Just a little note ♪ to let
you know how blessed I feel
to have had your presence on
my album. You truly are an
amazing musician Joeie ~ + God's
favor was upon me when he
wove you into my life!
Wishing you Blessings + Miracles..
w/ Love, Janie ♪ 😊

Leap of Faith

8 Daily Habits to Power Up Your Leap

Janie Lidey

Foreword by Glenn Morshower

Published by
Duswalt Press
280 N. Westlake Blvd
Westlake Village, CA 91362
Suite 110
www.duswaltpress.com

Manufactured in the United States of America, or in
the United Kingdom when distributed elsewhere.

Author: Lidey, Janie
Title: Leap of Faith ~ 8 Daily Habits to Power Up Your Leap
ISBN:
Paperback: 9781938015458
eBook: 9781938015465

Cover design by: Joe Potter
Cover photo by: Val Westover
Interior design: Scribe Inc.
Photo credits: Val Westover

Author's URL: www.janielidey.com

~ In loving memory of my dad ~

Charles Augustus Sykes
July 12, 1930–May 10, 2016

I dedicate this book to my husband, Sean, and our
son, Tristan. You have loved and supported me
without condition on my journey to lift people up and
help them grow their wings. Thank you for leaping
with faith and believing in my dream of raising
the vibration of love on our beautiful planet.

~ I love you MASS ~

Contents

Acknowledgments

The things I write about could not come from a heart untouched by God's love and the love of humankind. I wish to express my deep love and appreciation for all who have helped me shine a brighter light.

To God—for loving me unconditionally and showering me with Your favor.

To Sean and Tristan—for being my superheroes.

To Mum and Dad—for being the most loving, nurturing, supportive parents a girl could ever ask for.

To my sister Kris, and her husband, Dave—for always welcoming me with open hearts and arms to my home-away-from-home.

To my brother Bill—for always making me feel like such a talented musician.

To my brother Bobby—for just being.

To my sister Sue—for helping me grow my wings.

To my sister Carol—for being my twin two years removed. Corny as it sounds, you complete me.

To Reeney O'Reilley—for being my soul sister.

To Skip Franklin—for believing in my dream.

To Craig Duswalt—for always making me feel like a rock star.

To my mastermind family—for your amazing love, support, and encouragement.

To Karen Strauss—for your love and support as my publisher.

To Joe Potter—for your amazing graphics.

To all my extended family and friends—I love you!

And thank you to my special guest authors for your grace and presence:

Larry Broughton
Carol Casas
Don Cromwell
Craig Duswalt
Maryann Ehmann
Skip Franklin
Charlie Hewitt
Stephanie Adriana Westover

Wishing you all blessings and miracles in your leap of faith.

Foreword by Glenn Morshower

The essence of a person leaks out of them in everything they do. This is neither a good thing nor a bad thing. It is simply a truth. The saying goes, "How we do anything is how we do everything." In other words, we put our metaphorical fingerprint on everything we touch and everyone we encounter. In her book *Leap of Faith*, Janie Lidey's essence spills out beautifully all over the pages. Knowing her for several years has created my consistent expectation of pure goodness, and now here it is in book form. This goodness grabs the reader's hand and walks them into a deeper experience of what it means to actually live with faith. To enter a modality where we leap from the mountaintops and grow wings on the way down. In life, we don't need it **all mapped out** for us. The magic is in the mystery. This allows us to act confidently, with a faith that moves forward, believing that a favorable outcome awaits us. We are shown time and time again that it is done unto us according to our faith. Does this mean that we get every little thing we wish for? Absolutely not! We are simply implementing **the law of thought equals outcome**. What we focus on increases exponentially. The team of writers who have contributed additional thoughts are all professionals in their own fields of endeavor. The combination of winning strategies offered here makes *Leap of Faith* an absolute must read.

Introduction

If you are right here, right now, I believe you are where you're supposed to be, when you're supposed to be there. The universe has a way of bringing us what we need to hear when we need to hear it.

When I look back on my own journey, I can't help but notice the gifts that have magically appeared for me when I needed an awakening of some kind. Messages from people all over the world have shown up in the form of a song, a quote, a book, a poem, or a conversation. We are all woven together by this seemingly invisible web, and the more we open ourselves up to the quiet power of the universe, the easier it is to wake up to who we really are and lean into our gift.

After teaching middle and high school choir and guitar for more than twenty-five years, I found myself sitting in front of my students one day, doing what I had always done but not being present while I did it. I was playing the bass line on the piano, singing a line out to the alto section, writing a pass for a student to go to the restroom . . . and all the while, I was thinking about a new song I wanted to write, a music festival I wanted to sing at, recording in Nashville, or speaking to a large audience. Something in me was stirring and shifting, and I wasn't living in the present with my students anymore. I loved those kids so deeply, was excited about inspiring them to step into their greatness, was passionate about creating top-level performing choirs, truly believed in modeling high expectations, and always felt like I was living my true purpose as a teacher. I was living an inspired life . . . until one day, I wasn't. It had slowly crept up on me, but suddenly it was apparent that I no longer felt passionate about my calling as a teacher in one school. I was convinced that it was time to step out of the safety and comfort of one building and make the world my classroom. I had a message inside of me that I wanted to sing and shout out to the whole universe. I needed to start living in the present again. I needed to step away from the safety of a job that I had done for twenty-six years. I needed to take a leap of faith!

During the course of my own awakening, *Leap of Faith: 8 Daily Habits to Power Up Your Leap* was born. As I share these quotes, stories, and songs with you, it is my deepest hope that they will help you live authentically, love without condition, calm your fear, power up your leap, lean into your gift, and realize the myriad of blessings and miracles that are magically and abundantly waiting to appear in your life.

Toward the end of each chapter, you will hear from some very special authors. They are people whom I have been empowered and inspired by in my life, and I have asked them to share one of their special stories with you.

I have included some Daily Habit Action Steps after each guest author's story, and finally, each chapter will end with a song. As I have leaned into my own gift as a songwriter, I have come to realize the power of music to raise your vibration, calm your fear, and power up your leap.

And now . . . leap away.

Imagine what a harmonious world it could be if every single person, both young and old shared a little of what he is good at doing.

~ Quincy Jones ~

About the Song "Leap of Faith"
I was inspired to write "Leap of Faith" the day after my husband, Sean, brought me home a beautiful painting of a mountain goat leaping from one sheer cliff to another, hanging in midair. At the bottom of the painting it simply says "FAITH." That was his way of giving me permission to retire early from my teaching job and take a "Leap of Faith."

Leap of Faith
Inspired by Sean Lidey
Music & Lyrics by Janie Lidey & Matt Wilder, BMI
©2013

If I had no fear if there was only love
I'd do all the things that I've been dreamin' of
And if I had no doubt if all I had was time
I would climb the highest mountain I could climb

And I'd take the leap of faith that I always wanted to
I would spread my wings and fly the
way that I was meant to do
I would be strong enough to call my own bluff
And make all the dreams that matter come true
I'm gonna take the leap of faith
Gonna take the leap of faith
Gonna take the leap of faith

If I were not afraid I wouldn't have a care
And I'd do all the things that I never dared
If there were no regrets no future and no past
I would live each day as if it were my last

And I'd take the leap of faith that I always wanted to
I would spread my wings and fly the
way that I was meant to do

I would be strong enough to call my own bluff
And make all the dreams that matter come true

I'm gonna climb the highest mountain
I've ever climbed before
I'm gonna spread my wings so I can soar
I'm gonna dare to reach for things I've
never dared to reach before
And I'm gonna do it all without a single fear

I'll take the leap of faith that I always wanted to
I'll spread my wings and fly the
way that I was meant to do
I'm gonna be strong enough to call my own bluff
And make all the dreams that matter come true
I'm gonna take the leap of faith
Gonna take the leap of faith
Gonna take the leap of faith

Act as If

Act as if! Act as if you're a wealthy man, rich already, and then you'll surely become rich. Act as if you have unmatched confidence and then people will surely have confidence in you. Act as if you have unmatched experience and then people will follow your advice. And act as if you are already a tremendous success, and as sure as I stand here today—you will become successful.
~ Jordan Belfort, *The Wolf of Wall Street* ~

Are you the kind of person who expects blessings and miracles every day, or are you the kind of person who lives in fear, allowing that inner voice that lives inside your head to dominate and lead you through your day?

This chapter is intended to help you gain insight into how you can use the *act as if* concept to help you say yes, figure things out as you go, and begin claiming your dreams rather than chasing them.

I learned very early in life that even though I felt like a blessings-and-miracles kind of girl most of the time, I definitely spent way too much time listening to that voice of fear inside my head. I also learned that when I put my stake in the ground and shut down that little voice, it allowed me to take huge leaps of faith. And with each leap I took, after a bit of scary hanging-in-midair time, I landed where I felt I was destined to be. With time and practice, my leaps have become much larger and my landing place much greater. The bigger the leap, the greater the possibilities on the other side.

Say Yes Now and Figure Things Out as You Go

When I graduated college with a degree in music education, I had two choices for employment. I could either take a safe, convenient job in Seattle, Washington, or I could take a giant leap of faith and accept a nine-week residency in the remote, fly-in only village of Kwigillingok, Alaska. If I took the job in Seattle, I would be teaching junior high and high school choir, which is what I had gotten my degree in. If I took the job in Kwigillingok, I would be teaching music to kids from ages three to eighteen, and I had no training in the area of early childhood or elementary music education. To make it an even bigger leap, many of the younger kids in the village didn't speak English, so I would be teaching ESL (English as a second language), which I also had no training in. Yikes!

Because I am the kind of person who expects blessings and miracles (I won't say that my inner voice didn't rear up and try to make me take the job in Washington), I decided to take the job in Alaska. I felt like if I took the job in Seattle, it would be the beginning of a safe and mediocre career. But if I took the job in the remote village in Alaska, it would be the beginning of a courageous and amazing journey. In the words of Martha Beck,

> *To live a life that is wrong for you is a form of dying. There are people who have lives that look perfect. They try to be happy, they believe they should be happy, they are trying to like it, but if it's off course from their north star, they aren't satisfied.*

So I decided to say yes, figure it out as I went, and *act as if* I knew what I was doing.

I figured that I could brush up on enough skills to teach the younger students before the job in Alaska started. I had a professor tell me something during my last semester of college that has stuck with me through the years. He said, "Develop a thirst for knowledge and spend your life quenching that thirst." So I began to quench my thirst by visiting as many elementary school music classrooms as I could, where I could absorb the greatness of experts and carry that greatness to the village. I asked each music teacher to share his or her three best activities with me, and I built myself a special little toolbox of fun and educational activities for the younger students.

> **Develop a Thirst for Knowledge and Spend Your Life Quenching That Thirst**

I also reminded myself that the thing that was more important than teaching the subject of music was teaching kids to live their lives with passion, kindness, love, hope, and gratitude. The most important lesson was to instill the belief in my students that they could be or do anything they dreamed or imagined. I knew my heart was ready for this teaching assignment, so all I really needed to do was gather a few extra musical activities for the younger kids and I'd be ready to go.

After becoming as much of an expert as one can in a very short time, I boarded a plane in sunny San Francisco, where I flew to Seattle, changed planes, and headed for Anchorage. There, I boarded a smaller plane from Anchorage to Bethel, where I changed planes again and boarded a little Cessna that took me out to the village of Kwigillingok, Alaska (a.k.a. Kwig). I hopped off the Cessna onto a dog sled pulled by a snow machine and was whisked off to my village housing on the banks of the Kuskokwim River. The temperature was nearly one hundred degrees colder in Kwig than it was just hours earlier when I left San Francisco. There were only a few hours of daylight at that time of year in Alaska, and what might have been a drive to school in a heated car (had I taken the job in Seattle) was instead a ride in the dark from one end of the village to the other on my snow machine in sub-zero temperatures. There was no running water in Kwig, so my bathroom consisted of a honey bucket next to my bed and a cold, wet cloth for bathing each day. And during my first few days in the village, I accidentally drank some water that I hadn't boiled long enough, so Montezuma's Revenge and I had a lovely stay together in Honey Bucket Land. Do ya think that inner voice reared up and said, "Maybe you should've taken the safe, mediocre job in Seattle?" You bet!

So why is any of this relevant to you? Because if you are right here, right now, it means you are either getting ready to go out on a limb or you have already taken a leap of faith and you are hanging in midair.

Now is a good time to remember that choosing the easy road is not usually the path to achieving your highest level of success and truly living your best life. Robert Frost put it so well when he said,

Two roads diverged in a wood and I—I took the one less traveled by, and that has made all the difference.

Claim Your Dreams Rather than Chasing Them

Half way through my nine-week residency in Kwig, the neighboring village of Kongiganak (a.k.a. Kong) heard of my program and asked if I would come teach in their village when I was done in Kwig. I had *acted as if* I had unmatched confidence, and people began to have confidence in me. I had *acted as if* I had unmatched experience, and people were following my advice. And I had *acted as if* I was already a tremendous success, and I had become successful. In fact, among other things, I was even being touted as a highly effective addition to the ESL program. I said yes, figured it out as I went, and I now had a tremendous start to my career. I was being sought after to teach in other villages, was offered $600 per week to teach my program, was provided free room and board and my own snow machine, and all flights to and from the villages were paid in full. Not bad for someone fresh out of college in 1985.

Once I began to feel the self-worth that came with this early success as a teacher, I decided to claim the next part of my dream. There were no music positions open in the Anchorage School District (where I wanted to live and teach), so I had to think outside the box and come up with a plan to continue the courageous and amazing journey I was on. I had seen a lot of young graduates in my field chasing their dreams but ending up as substitute teachers and having to wait tables on the side to make ends meet. That just didn't feel right for me. I knew that there was a need for music in the village schools and that a lot of the bush areas in Alaska did not have a full-time music teacher. I also knew that the North Slope of Alaska had a nice budget overflow due to the oil revenues the state had been experiencing. I was so passionate about this exciting career and the impact I had on the students in Kwig and Kong, and I wanted to continue on this amazing journey. So I decided to claim my dream. I wrote up a proposal and sent it to the superintendent of the North Slope Borough School District, described what I had to offer, attached some amazing letters of recommendation from the principals in Kwig and Kong (always get testimonials along your way) and asked for the following:

- $1,000 a week
- All travel expenses paid for getting to and from the villages
- Six weeks on, one week off
- Room and board

At the age of twenty-four, my proposal was accepted, and I took another big leap of faith, moved to Anchorage, bought a house, and began my journey to and from the North Slope of Alaska.

Always Get Testimonials along the Way

A Sample of One of My Most Favorite Testimonials

May 4, 2014
To Whom It May Concern:

It is an honor to be asked to write this letter of support for Janie Lidey. I've known Janie for many years, having become a school administrator at East High in 1996, where she was teaching choir and other music classes until 2011 when she retired to pursue writing, performing, and sharing her music with an even wider audience. I've had the opportunity to observe first hand her organizational skills and effectiveness in working with students, her ability to inspire others, and her amazing ability to positively connect with everyone from young people to senior citizens within an incredibly diverse community.

As a high school music teacher, everything Janie touched or did turned to gold. Students were absolutely drawn to her. Beyond the musical accolades and excellence Janie cultivated at East, her greatest strength was an almost magical ability to connect with students from every walk of life, inspiring them to believe in themselves and their ability to make a positive difference in the world. She not only managed to make them better musicians, she made them want to be better people. She inspires confidence, trust and respect from others, which in turn allows her to have a positive impact and to help them grow. While it was a blow to East High when she announced she was retiring from her teaching position, she was doing so to pursue her dream of sharing her gifts and positive message with a wider audience, and she was greatly respected for it. She served and continues to serve as a model for those with a dream.

Janie's music has also had a deep impact on others. Her music and legacy live on at East Anchorage High School where her Emmy Award winning "Change of Heart" song continues to be a popular and meaningful theme song that expresses the acceptance students have for one another in what was recently declared to be the most diverse high school student body in the United States. Indeed, Janie has the gift of taking any idea or situation, understanding what's really important in it, and turning it into music with a message that penetrates to the heart of the matter, as well as the heart of her listeners.

Sincerely,
Michael T. Graham
Chief Academic Officer,
Anchorage School District
Former Principal of East High

Acting as if and claiming my dream took me on a journey far beyond my wildest expectations. That initial leap of faith brought me down a path that opened up doors, allowing me the opportunity to eventually teach at a Fine Arts School of Choice in Anchorage, Alaska, where I became a highly sought after leader in my community and got to work on a team that led our school to winning a Grammy Award. It's funny—there was a highly qualified teacher from Seattle who applied for the job, but I believe that my decision to *act as if*, leap with faith, and choose the courageous and amazing journey of teaching in the Alaskan bush schools set me apart from a candidate that chose the safer job in Seattle.

And now I'd like to introduce you to my good friend and mentor, Craig Duswalt. Craig was the former personal assistant for Axl Rose of Guns N' Roses and also toured with Air Supply for many years. I met him at his popular RockStar Marketing BootCamp in Los Angeles, California, and I chose Craig to be my special guest author for the "Act as If" chapter because he is a master at helping people realize the power of acting as if, saying yes, and figuring it out as you go.

Craig Duswalt

Here are two of my mantras: "Say **yes** and figure it out later" and "Act as if."

"Say **yes** and figure it out later" has gotten me booked on stages all across America, because the event planners who hire me know that I will make it happen, no matter what the circumstances.

But "Act as if" has helped me create a career.

When I was a kid, I used to pretend (as all kids do) that I was a pitcher in the major leagues, pitching with two outs in the bottom of the ninth inning of the World Series, and there were two strikes on the batter I was facing. I would visualize standing on the mound in front of sixty-five thousand screaming fans, taking a deep breath, then throwing my fastball as hard as I could and watching the batter swing and miss. The crowd would go crazy, and my teammates would carry me off the field on their shoulders.

My vivid imagination helped me "act as if" it really happened, and I was able to feel what I thought it would feel like. It was amazing.

I did that my entire life, not only with sports but also with getting a lead in a movie (I was an actor at one point in my life) and singing on stage with the band Queen (I'm a huge Queen fan).

And then I grew up, and "acting as if" became the knowledge that I could create outer circumstances by "acting as if" they were already real.

So when I got the job as the band assistant for the very popular band Air Supply two weeks out of college, I really wasn't surprised it happened. I visualized that great things were going to happen to me because I had a lot of energy, had a very positive attitude, and was very confident.

In order to be successful in this type-A personality, success-driven world, you must have confidence. Even if you have low self-esteem, you must at least "act as if" you have a ton of confidence.

"Act as if" took an interesting turn while I was on tour with Air Supply in the late eighties and when I toured with Guns N' Roses as Axl Rose's personal assistant in the early nineties. I saw firsthand what was now possible if you were able to just "act as if."

When I toured with Air Supply and Guns N' Roses, I noticed how hard it was for a fan to get backstage during a show. Between the huge bodyguards who toured with us and the enormous security guards employed by the venue, it was virtually impossible.

So in order for us to stand out from the fans, we all wore laminated passes clipped to lanyards around our necks, and these passes gave us All Access to anywhere in the venue. All we had to do was flash our laminated pass, and we could get past any security guard in the building.

Yet if you didn't have that silly little laminated pass around your neck, there was no way you were getting backstage . . . unless you were a really beautiful woman. But that's a whole other story.

But then . . .

One night, somewhere on the East Coast, I was out in the crowd, saying hi to some friends while Air Supply was on stage. There must have been about twenty thousand crazed fans in the audience. As the show came to a close, I headed toward the backstage area to get drinks and towels ready for the band when they came off stage. But as I walked past the security guard to get backstage, he stopped me. I reached for my laminated pass around my neck to show him who I was, and it wasn't there. I forgot it backstage.

I tried to explain to the security guard that I was with the band, and he calmly shared with me that he had heard that same story about fifty times that evening from other people trying to get backstage to meet the band.

Ugh.

I immediately tried to get someone's attention backstage, but the music was too loud. And now time was running out—I had to get backstage fast to prep for the encore.

I ran to the other side of the stage and decided to go for it again, but this time I would walk with a purpose, walk past this new security guard with confidence, and **not** make eye contact. I would walk right past him, "acting as if" I was supposed to be going backstage to handle something very important.

And that's what I did. As Janie's book title says, I took a "leap of faith."

And it worked. I walked right past him. Didn't look back, just kept going.

I "acted as if" I was supposed to be there.

It's that simple.

Janie shared with her students the idea that they could be or do anything they dreamed or imagined. In 2006, I dreamt of becoming a professional speaker. It was just a "dream," but I knew I was armed with forty-six years of amazing life experiences that I could share from the stage, and I "imagined" that people would listen.

Today, I "act as if" I'm a successful speaker, and guess what? I have a successful speaking career. It's that simple.

Daily Habit Action Steps

- What will you do today to *act as if*?

- What can you say yes to now and figure out as you go?

- What are you doing to quench your thirst for knowledge?

- What are doing to claim your dreams rather than chasing them?

- Whom could you get to write a testimonial for you?

About the Song "I Don't Wanna Go Slow"
"I Don't Wanna Go Slow" was inspired by my husband, Sean. He loves to buy old classic muscle cars, fix them up, and then sell them. One day, I realized how sexy it was that I always got to go for at least one ride in them before they went up for sale, and suddenly this song just came pouring out.

The reason I am sharing it with you at the end of my "Act as If" chapter is that when I decided to retire early and go to Nashville, I *acted as if* I were going to meet all the people I had dreamed of meeting and *acted as if* blessings and miracles were going to happen while I was there. When I asked my producer, Matt Wilder, whom I could get to record my duet with me, he contacted none other than Faith Hill's backup singer Perry Coleman. Faith has been on my dream board for years, and now I am singing "I Don't Wanna Go Slow" with a member of her band.

The More You *Act as If*, the Smaller the Degrees of Separation between You and Your Dreams

I Don't Wanna Go Slow
Inspired by Sean Lidey
Music & Lyrics by Janie Lidey & Matt Wilder, BMI
©2013

I woke up 6 a.m. had no place to go
So I had a cup of coffee and listened to the radio
But when I turned that stereo on they
were playin' our favorite song
And suddenly I couldn't get to you fast
enough 'cause baby with you

I don't wanna go slow I just wanna lose control
I don't wanna think twice I just wanna be by your side
You make me wanna speed up you
make me wanna fly so high
So drive me like a fast car pedal to the
metal and take me for a ride
'Cause I don't want to go slow

Got on the freeway to go to work another day
Got stuck in the slow lane and turned the radio on
And there it was our favorite song I wished
you were ridin' along with me
So we could race on down that old
back road 'cause baby with you

I don't wanna go slow I just wanna lose control
I don't wanna think twice I just wanna be by your side
You make me wanna speed up you
make me wanna fly so high
So drive me like a fast car pedal to the
metal and take me for a ride
'Cause I don't want to go slow

Kiss me harder love me stronger
than you think you should
Hold me tighter take me deeper
than you thought you could

'Cause I don't wanna go slow I just wanna lose control
I don't wanna think twice I just wanna be by your side
You make me wanna speed up you
make me wanna fly so high
So drive me like a fast car pedal to the
metal, and take me for a ride
'Cause I don't want to go slow
I don't wanna go slow
I don't wanna go slow

Begin It Now

*Whatever you can do or dream you can, begin it. Boldness
has genius, power and magic in it. Begin it now!*
~ Johann Wolfgang von Goethe ~

What do you do when you are faced with a difficult life
choice? Do you ever hear those whispers that make you
feel as though you are supposed to shift? Are you the
kind of person who listens to those whispers and then
boldly begins the steps in the direction of your dream,
or are you the one who just plays it safe and stays put?

This chapter is intended to help you gain insight into
how you can use the *begin it now* concept to ignite the
energy of the universe to help bring a myriad of things
your way, whether with baby steps or giant leaps.

When I began to feel as though I was supposed to
shift after twenty-six years of teaching music in Alaska,

I knew I would have to calm my fear and figure out a way to start taking steps toward my destiny. My heart kept telling me to be bold and leap with faith, but that inner voice kept telling me to stay put and play it safe. I had taught music in the remote villages for three years; did one year of elementary classroom music; spent five years teaching middle school choir and guitar; and had been teaching a combination of choir, guitar, and keyboard at the high school level for seventeen years. I loved my job and my students, but I just kept feeling this sense of a whisper in my heart, which soon became a shout, saying, "Step out of the safety and comfort of your classroom, and make the world your classroom!" After witnessing the positive effect I was having on my students over the years, I felt a responsibility to see if I might be able to have a positive impact on a global level.

Even though I had the option to take an early retirement and actually collect a small pension and benefits for my family, I kept hearing that inner voice saying, "Are you crazy? If you retire now, you won't have enough money to pay your bills! If you just go five more years—or better yet, ten more years—then you'll have a decent pension!"

So what do you do when you are faced with a difficult life choice? You go back to *acting as if,* and you *begin it now*!

I decided to go home from school one day and share my desire to shift with my husband. I figured he would either tell me not to quit my day job or encourage me to go for it and we would figure it out as we went. Thankfully, he went out the next day and bought me that beautiful piece of artwork I mentioned earlier, with the mountain goat powerfully leaping from one sheer cliff to another, surely to fall to its death were it not to make the other side, and the caption at the bottom that simply says "FAITH."

Don't Be Afraid to Shift If That Is What Your Heart Is Telling You to Do

When I fully realized that I was meant to shift, I decided to look at some of the things I could do to begin the process. I knew that if I were to *act as if* and begin to take even some tiny steps to *begin it now*, it would ignite the quiet power of the universe, and my new path would begin to appear.

Here is where I want to stress to you the importance of realizing that, whether through giant leaps or tiny steps, you can create your reality by taking action.

I will give you a few samples of the actions I took to *begin it now*, and then I will share how the universe supported me on my journey:

- I began cleaning out my closet and bagged up all the school clothing that I had accumulated over seventeen years at East High, and I labeled the bags with the following:
  - All choir director clothing: Donate to the new choir director who will be replacing me when I retire early.
  - All staff clothing: Donate to the new faculty members who sometimes can't afford the staff shirts.
  - All choir T-shirts, sweat shirts, sweat pants: Bring to school and donate to students who can't afford to buy their own.

I did all this with the intention of not needing any of my East High School attire anymore because I would be taking an early retirement. I kept one or two items for nostalgia and bagged up the rest. I took a few other steps as well:

- I began cleaning up my office and music library as though I would be prepping for a new choir teacher to take my job.
- I began secretly looking for a new choir director to replace me.
- I got online and downloaded the early retirement forms. (Even though I didn't send them in right away, I filled them out as if I were retiring now.)

Be Bold! Whether Giant Leaps or Baby Steps, You Can Create Your Reality by Taking Action

It wasn't long after *acting as if* and *beginning it now* that I started to see signs of the shift happening. Blessings and miracles began to materialize, and before I knew it, I had not only found a highly qualified choir director to take my place at East High, but in addition to that, my husband came into a little bit of money by complete surprise, which allowed us to calm some of the fear we had about the reduction in pay we would experience during this shift. Suddenly, I found myself *really* taking the leap of faith and submitting my retirement paper work. The question I asked myself at this juncture was, "Would these blessings and miracles have happened had I not taken the steps to *begin it now*?"

Johann Wolfgang Von Goethe says,

Until one is committed, there is hesitancy, the chance to draw back, always ineffectiveness, concerning all acts of initiative (and creation). There is one elementary truth the ignorance of which kills countless ideas and splendid plans: that the moment one definitely commits oneself then Providence moves too. All sorts of things occur to help one that would never have occurred. A whole stream of events issues from the decision, raising in one's favor all manner of unforeseen incidents and meetings and material assistance which no man would have dreamed would have come his way. Whatever you can do or dream you can, begin it. Boldness has genius, power and magic in it. Begin it now.

And now I'd like to introduce you to my beautiful friend Stephanie Adriana Westover, who has become an honorary sister in my family. Stephanie is a former model and now, alongside her husband, Val, she is the owner of Capturing True Emotion. I chose Stephanie to be my special guest author for the "Begin It Now" chapter because she and Val could be the poster children for stepping out in faith and boldly beginning the things they dream of.

Stephanie Adriana Westover

There's no time like the present
No present like time
And life can be over in the space of a rhyme.

~ Georgia Byng ~

Life will throw you curve balls, some good and some bad. Realizing the opportunity in the curve ball is where the gift is. Life is simply an enormous opportunity, and seeing the positive, rather than the negative, will always benefit you. Make every moment count and *begin it now*.

When I was in the tenth grade, I severely disliked school. Because it wasn't my favorite endeavor, I decided to take the California Proficiency Exam and leave high school to go to junior college (or at least that's what I convinced my parents I was going to do). A month later, I did a photo shoot with a friend who was trying to get signed to a modeling agency. She didn't want to do it alone, so I went with her and I ended up getting signed on too. So I shifted out of the college scene, became an emancipated minor, and threw myself head over heels into my first big *begin it now*.

Modeling was fun, exciting, and difficult all at the same time. Even though I'd be modeling a cool product in a fun place with interesting people, there were many long hours, uncomfortable situations, and extreme personalities. The majority of the time, it was not as glamorous as it is made out to be, but I am very lucky and blessed to have learned patience and developed the tremendous ability to handle difficult situations. Making the decision to just be bold and begin something new gave me some very cool real-life problem-solving and people-handling superpowers.

I thought that modeling would be my career until I met a man named Val Westover. Val was a very successful portrait photographer in Orange County in early 2000, and his business was booming. Photographing five to eight sessions a day, Val was almost faced with more than he could handle.

After a day of modeling, I found it fun to assist Val with lighting a photo shoot on the beach. At first, I was more than happy to hold the screen/light diffuser, shading Val's clients while staring out at the ocean and watching dolphins go by. But then all of a sudden, I started paying more attention and actually participated in the session by helping with setup and working with the families. One evening, on the way to the beach, we stopped off at Val's studio for some props. While waiting, I was privy to a conversation Val's secretary was having with a client. The client asked if Val photographed weddings, and the receptionist said that he did not. Val was too busy with multiple sessions during the day to take the time to photograph one single wedding.

On the car ride to our next beach session, I asked Val if he would consider teaching me photography so that he would not have to give potential wedding shoots away. Val admitted that he never wanted to have an assistant or teach another person because he was afraid to give his secrets and knowledge away only to have the trainee leave and start their own business. With a little convincing and big toothy grins, I had Val feeling secure that I would try my best to learn the business and then apply my new craft to benefitting *his* business. After two years of shooting side by side, I felt confident enough to take on my own clients by myself and, more important, to take on Val's clients. In 2008, I photographed thirty-eight weddings and found that I absolutely loved the chaos, pressure, emotion, and potential beauty of a wedding. But little did we know that this was the beginning of the steady decline of our business due to the economic crash that started in 2008.

While Val was feeling the pain from the lack of business in 2009, I decided to say yes to an invitation from our very close friends, Kail and Renee Mantle, and go to Montana to participate in their world-famous annual horse drive. During this incredible event, I learned so many amazing things. I learned that I love documenting the moment. I learned that I have a definite talent for capturing horses and landscape. And I came away with the image of my life, "The Round Up," which, in 2010, was featured in *Cowboys & Indians* magazine as its equine photo of the year. This was a cool and enormous accolade but not strong enough to change the tide of the 2008 economic fiasco.

From 2009 to 2010, I watched Val frantically trying to market and solicit clients who no longer could afford his luxury product. He decided to try something new and began sending out e-mails, mailers, and ads in magazines, giving their recipients the deal of the century. He didn't realize the myriad of things that would come his way by just beginning something new, but Val was creating his ticket to the future. During all this advertising, he started receiving requests from his clients to privately teach them how to use their own cameras. This dismayed Val because he thought that he was training his clients to photograph their own families and that he was teaching himself straight out of a job. But after he would teach one client, they would call and ask Val if he would teach five of their friends together in a group.

Then God, the Universe, or some amazing energy force decided to throw us another curve ball. Val saw the gift in it, took that ball, and ran with it!

It began with an invitation I got to attend a seminar on how to write a book in thirty days. I dragged Val with me just for the heck of it, and this became a turning point in Val's career. He was so inspired by this incredible system for writing a book that the moment he got home, he implemented the *begin it now* theory, and in roughly thirty days, he became the author of *Understanding the Basic Elements of Photography.*

Val was now armed with this incredible teaching and promotional tool. He then created a workbook that aided in teaching his private students. Because of this book and his new fame for teaching photography, a new, small Internet-based company you may have heard of called Groupon approached Val. They were running a one-deal-a-day program, and he had twenty-four hours to take advantage of the offer. Val accepted it even though we had a little logistical problem. It was a Groupon sales associate from Arizona who wanted to know if Val would teach photography in Tucson. Val decided to use the "just say yes and figure it out as you go" theory, and that **yes** was our biggest *begin it now* ever.

We sold over 400 Groupon coupons in Tucson, followed by 2,500 in Phoenix and 2,300 in Houston. And as they say, "Houston, we have a problem." Though we saw it not as a problem, but an enormous opportunity! Val asked me if I would take the show on the road with him, and I just said, "Yes!" We decided to *begin it now,* and we had the most crazy, wonderful, awesome two-and-a-half years traveling to over twenty cities in the United States, teaching over twenty-three thousand people in-person.

In 2012, we evolved our successful live workshop into an online course that over ten thousand people are currently taking, and we are not stopping there. Another *begin it now* is around the corner for us with the launch of my book, *The Creative Photographer*. And after that, the sky's the limit.

Sometimes we can't see what is right in front of us, and objects that we *can* see seem bigger than they are. This can leave us overwhelmed. But you are the captain of your own ship. You are in charge of your own destiny. Dream of your perfect future and believe that you can make it happen. Like Janie said, be bold! Whether through great leaps or baby steps, you can create your reality by taking action. So take advantage of every curve ball that life throws you and make it into the best *begin it now* opportunity ever!

Daily Habit Action Steps

• What can you do today to *begin it now* and start claiming your dream?

• Are you hearing any "whispers" in your head about wanting to shift? Write them down, *act as if,* and *begin it now.*

• List some baby steps that you could take now to start shifting.

• List some great leaps that you could take now to start shifting. **Be bold** and let that negative inner voice know that it is not welcome on this journey.

About the Song "Abundance"

This song came to life at a faith-based event in Coronado Bay, California. Maryann Ehmann invited me to sing and speak at her annual event, "Create Your Magnificent Year," and while there, one of the attendees, my good friend Cindy Baldwin, reached over and handed me a few lines of a poem she had written that morning. I took those lines and created this song for the final morning of our seminar. The reason I am sharing this song with you at the end of my "Begin It Now" chapter is that it is all about how we create our day rather than our day creating us. It is in the here and now that we use our power to create our own reality by boldly stepping out in faith to "Begin It Now."

Abundance
Inspired by Cindy Baldwin,
Maryann Ehmann & Nick Castellano
Music by Janie Lidey, BMI
Lyrics by Cindy Baldwin & Janie Lidey
©2016

Abundance does grow on trees
It runs in the grass and it swims in the seas
It is the ocean the sun and the breeze
Abundance does grow on trees

Create you day rather than your day creating you
Abundance does grow on trees
Blessings and miracles every single day
Abundance does grow on trees

We create our own reality
We can be a mighty oak if that is
what we're called to be
We are royal we are epic beyond our wildest dreams

It's in the now we have the power
Every minute of every hour
When that power is lined up with
what we're called to do
It's in the now we have the power

Create you day rather than your day creating you
Abundance does grow on trees
Blessings and miracles every single day
Abundance does grow on trees

We create our own reality
We can be a mighty oak if that is
what we're called to be
We are royal we are epic beyond our wildest dreams

Abundance does grow on trees
Abundance does grow on trees
Abundance does grow on trees

Dream Big

The future belongs to those who believe in the beauty of their dreams.

~ Eleanor Roosevelt ~

Is there something in your heart that you have been dreaming about for a long time but haven't had the courage to bring about? Do you spend time daydreaming about things you would love to see happen in your life but never go beyond the daydream and actually claim those dreams?

Remember that there is a big difference between chasing your dreams and claiming your dreams!

This chapter is intended to help you gain insight into how you can use the *dream big* concept to help you decide that your dream is important, claim that dream, create dream boards that bring life to your dream before it has even become real, and then live your life on purpose.

Decide That Your Dream Is Important

The story I am about to share is a direct result of what happens when you decide that your dream is important enough to get out your dream board and create a visual tapestry that helps you live your dream before it has even become real.

Before I met my husband, Sean, I bought a little three-bedroom ranch house that was the perfect size for my cat, Kuniaq (meaning "Little Hunter," named after one of my students in the village of Nuiqsut on the North Slope), and me to live in. After meeting Sean; bringing our new puppy, Kodiak, home; and having our son, Tristan, that little ranch home became rather crowded. As our family grew, so too did our dreams about the kind of home we would like to live in.

Both Sean and I had always dreamed of living in a log home. We couldn't afford to make that dream come true during those younger years, so we decided to go out and buy a big dream board so that our vision became real to us even if it was only on paper. We started cutting out pictures from log home magazines and created a dream board that we would look at each day and add to as we found things that we both liked and could picture being in our home. We also started going to Home Depot and Lowes and checking out all the different kinds of tile, woodworking, appliances, and paint colors that we would put in our home if we were building it already. When we found something we liked, we added it to the board.

The more we focused on our dream board, the more fired up we got about actually building our dream home. In fact, we were so excited that we decided to start driving around the hillside each night after dinner, just looking to see if a piece of land might come up for sale that was affordable enough for us to build on. After a few months of seeing nothing but land that was way outside our budget and realizing how many of those properties had covenants against building a log structure, we began to feel a little bit discouraged. But we kept the dream alive by continuing to build our dream board and manifest. One day, my realtor called us and said that a piece of property had just come on the market that morning, and it sounded perfect for us. We drove straight up the hill to take a look, and sure enough, it was perfect. It was almost half the cost of all the other properties we had seen; it was backed up to a greenbelt with a view of Denali, Mount Susitna, and the Chugach Mountains; and there were no covenants about what kind of home could be built in the subdivision.

Here is where I want to share the magic of *acting as if, beginning it now,* and *dreaming big.* The day before Sean and I found the perfect piece of land on which to build our perfect log home, I got a check for $15,000 to cover the costs of injuries sustained in a car accident that took place the previous year. I had no idea that I was going to get any kind of settlement at all from the accident, but I literally had a check in my wallet that morning that was the exact amount we needed for the down payment on the land. So we offered full price, it was accepted, and within hours our realtor was calling us with offers from other buyers who wanted the property. Apparently, the people who sold it to us had lived out of state for over twenty years and didn't realize the value of their land. We got it for a steal, and now we could focus on manifesting the money to actually build our dream home.

Create a Visual Tapestry That Helps You Live Your Dream before It Has Even Become Real

The economy had changed a bit for the better since I had bought my little ranch house. Now that we had the property secured for building our new log home, we started brainstorming on how to claim that next stage of our dream. We decided to list our house as for sale by owner and see if we could make enough to raise the seed money for the log kit we had chosen, which was $50,000. And then I began to imagine having someone come look at the house right away and offer us the full price we were asking. I had begun to understand so much about how to power up my leap over the years, and I knew that I could use its power to bring about this next phase of our journey. I started *acting as if* the house was already sold, packed up things and got them ready to move, and then posted the home for sale on Craigslist. We hung signs around town advertising our open house, baked bread so that the house smelled delicious to anyone who came by, and before the week was up, we had a buyer. The amazing thing was that she said she wasn't even in the market to buy a new house, but she saw our signs and something just made her come take a look. She fell in love with our little place and offered us our full asking price. We walked away the next week with a check for $50,000. Once again, I found myself asking the question, "Would these things have happened had I not allowed myself *to act as if, begin it now,* and *dream big*?"

And now I'd like to introduce you to my dear friend Maryann Ehmann. Maryann is a lifestyle business mentor, speaker, and author whom I chose to be my special guest author for the "Dream Big" chapter because she has inspired me to lean in closer to God and know that His favor is helping me activate my dreams and create my magnificent life.

Maryann Ehmann

Honoring our dreams and deciding they matter is a necessary practice in fulfilling our dreams. Thank you, Janie, for pointing that out. As a professional dream activator and facilitator, I have no doubt about the significance of this. But one of the things I have discovered is that most people do not know they have dreams worth honoring, or if they do, they have little clarity as to what they are. To dream is a huge challenge for some, let alone to *dream big*. However, as I will show you, to dream is to live.

There are many obstacles to seeing our dreams, let alone realizing them. Many of us are in survival mode, which can totally obscure our dreams, or we may have good lives and feel guilty wanting more, and then again, there are those who have been so wounded in life that cynicism aims to protect them from ever being disappointed. To not dream seems safer and "wiser" than taking the chance on folly. Other obstacles that can muddy the waters are over-responsibility and a deep belief of unworthiness. I had all the above, and I didn't even know it until May of 2005.

It was a cool spring evening and one of our favorite speakers had come into town to speak at our little country church. His stories as to what God was doing in other parts of the world were often fascinating and opened our eyes beyond our daily concerns. His inspiring words of wisdom and truth often challenged the limitations of our minds and courage. It was after one of these messages that he approached my husband and me and declared, almost out of nowhere, that God had seen the dreams that we had shelved and was activating them now, and we would activate the dreams of others. Further, we would be brought into financial freedom and lead others to it as well.

My husband smiled thoughtfully. I doubled over, as if punched in the gut, and sobbed. Uncontrollably. Dreams? What dreams? Activate them in others? How would that ever happen if I didn't even have any myself?

I was a busy homeschooling mom who had left a career as an attorney and financial adviser to be home with my children—and, if truth be known, to escape the corporate world and all its politics and striving. To have a career that provided prestige, power, and financial gain was my dream. I had achieved it, but not without oppressive stress from endless demands as well as the clear expectation that I was to have no life outside of work. Eventually, I had to get out.

My dreams had always related to my career, and without that, my dreaming seemed to stop. However, once I no longer struggled with the stigma of being "just" a stay-at-home mom, I discovered it was the best career of my life. Beyond my dreams. But then one year turned into another, and I discovered something else: I carried the same high-achieving striving into my role as supermom, and super-Christian, and superleader, and . . . Responsibility became my middle name. Living on one income became a challenge as well, so anything extra was out of the question. And there was the church community. Wherever we moved, and whatever church we were in, somehow I became one of the primary counselors—and sometimes the only one. My phone rang off the hook, I had trouble saying "no," and eventually, rather than be grateful to be used by God, I felt abused by Him and others, and a series of burnouts transpired.

Despite this, we had a good life. And to want more seemed greedy. So if more good things happened, it would have been a happy treat, but to purposely dream, and dream big? Who does that? It just seemed like a lot of pop psychology that smarter people like me didn't fall for. And here was this man, peering deep into my soul, speaking these words that pierced the depths of my heart, causing me to see with excruciating accuracy that I had stopped dreaming. But even more, though I no longer dreamed, my dreams still existed, and new life was being breathed into them. They were being "activated."

Now, I have to say, it would be years before I clarified my dreams and decided they were important and would come to fruition. One by one, perceived obstacles and limitations had to be removed. A new identity of worth and value had to be established, and God and I did that together. Daring to dream became my reality, and a warrior-like determination to walk in the favor of God rather than the fear of everything became my focused purpose.

Since then, it's utterly amazing the dreams that have come true . . . taking family trips to England, Italy, and more; having all four children married to spouses who are perfect for them; meeting the right people at the right time in the right place to help me with each of my dreams; and best of all, creating a dream-coaching and speaking business that I can do from anywhere, at any time, and with anyone.

Dreaming has become a habit now. But also exciting, there is immeasurably more beyond my dreams that, by the grace of God, I see manifest regularly.

There is a passage in the Bible that says, "Without a vision (or dream, in the Hebrew), people perish." I didn't know a part of me was dying and needed to be enlivened and activated. Maybe that's the case with you, too. If you feel you have stopped dreaming, or your dreams aren't clear, or that there are too many obstacles to them being fulfilled, may I encourage you? You already came prepacked with dreams. God made you that way. And if so, the way to fulfill them already exists. Take a step. Do as Janie suggested: decide your dreams are important, honor them with dream boards, and move forward. See your dreams come to life. It's the only way to **live**.

Daily Habit Action Steps

- Decide that your dream is important. Then begin to visualize the kind of dream board you could build.

- Go out today and buy a dream board and some magazines. Begin to cut out pictures of things that you have been dreaming about, and create a visual tapestry for your dream.

- What is the life of your dreams? What are you going to do today to bring yourself closer to living that life?

About the Song "Back to the Garden"
When Maryann Ehmann invited me to sing and speak at her "Create Your Magnificent Year" event in 2015, she added me to the group e-mail she was sending out to the folks who were going to be attending her event. The wisdom Maryann shared in those emails got me so fired up that this song just came spilling out of me. I include it at the end of my "Dream Big" chapter because it is all about dreaming as big as you can dream and blazing from within.

Back to the Garden
Inspired by Maryann Ehmann & Marcus Slaton
Music & Lyrics by Janie Lidey, BMI
©2014

Time goes by and life rolls on
But every day is right here and is
right now before it's gone

So I'm gonna live it out
I'm gonna sing and shout
And I'm gonna put my stake in the ground
I'm gonna dream as big as I can dream
Blazing from within
I'm gonna get myself back to the garden

I'm gonna fly so high and even if I fall
I'm not gonna fade away
I'm not gonna live my life as a flower on the wall

I'm gonna live it out
I'm gonna sing and shout
And I'm gonna put my stake in the ground
I'm gonna dream as big as I can dream
Blazing from within
I'm gonna get myself back to the garden

Round and round we go
Up and down and side to side
Spinning like a Ferris wheel
And sometimes it's like we're riding on
a wild and crazy rollercoaster ride

I'm gonna live it out
I'm gonna sing and shout
And I'm gonna put my stake in the ground
I'm gonna dream as big as I can dream
Blazing from within
I'm gonna get myself back to the garden . . . once again

Just Imagine

Imagination is everything. It is the preview of life's coming attractions.

~ Albert Einstein ~

What if you were told that your dreams could come true if you only took the time each day to imagine what they looked like? And what if that truth became even more solid if you were to actually feel what those dreams felt like as though they already had come true?

Bob Proctor says, "What you think about, you bring about." If you had a magic wand and you could do anything you wanted to in life, what would it be? If you had no fear, no doubt, no financial restrictions, what would your dream life look like? If you could take a leap of faith and run toward what you feel most passionate about, where would you be, what would you be doing, how would you feel, and who would be by your side?

This chapter is intended to help you gain insight into how you can use the *just imagine* habit to bring your dreams to life by allowing your thoughts to create your reality.

Throughout history, statements have been made by some of the most amazing human beings regarding the power of imagination.

Imagination is the beginning of creation. You imagine what you desire, you will what you imagine and at last you create what you will.
~ George Bernard Shaw ~

To bring anything into your life, imagine that it's already there.
~ Richard Bach ~

We do not need magic to change the world, we carry all the power we need inside ourselves already: we have the power to imagine better.
~ J. K. Rowling ~

You can't depend on your eyes when your imagination is out of focus.

~ Mark Twain ~

Live out of your imagination, not your history.

~ Stephen Covey ~

Without leaps of imagination or dreaming, we lose the excitement of possibilities. Dreaming, after all, is a form of planning.

~ Gloria Steinem ~

The man who has no imagination has no wings.

~ Muhammad Ali ~

Imagination Makes Your Dreams Come True

The power we each possess to create our reality through the use of our imagination is real. What you spend your time thinking about is what you end up bringing about. People who have made it to the very top in their careers have said when asked how it felt to be there, "It felt exactly how it did when I imagined it this way over and over again." I like to say that imagination makes your dreams come true.

When I took the leap of faith and retired early from teaching, I truly wanted to make the world my classroom. I wanted to use my music and message to help people raise their vibration and live their best life. Because I am a little bit country, my husband encouraged me to travel to Nashville and spend some time *acting as if* I were already living that dream. So I packed up my guitar and headed for Tennessee. Before my travels, I spent time imagining what kinds of things I'd like to see happen while there, and then I tried to feel what those things felt like as though they were already real. I knew that I could have a bigger impact on the world if I had a bigger following, and to have a bigger following, it seemed like I should connect with some people who had built a name for themselves in the music industry. So I imagined connecting and networking with folks who were hit songwriters, famous artists, or people who worked alongside famous artists.

One day, after a good session with my imagination, I decided to just show up on music row in downtown Nashville and expect blessings and miracles to happen. I had met a songwriter named Aaron who invited me to stop by his writing room anytime, and I figured today was a good day to do so. While visiting with Aaron, a gentleman named Wood Newton, who had a studio right across the hall from Aaron, dropped in to let us know that his writing appointment with someone had turned into a no show. Aaron told Wood about me and asked if he would be willing to do a co-write with a songwriter from Alaska. When I first walked into Wood's office, he hadn't really committed to writing with me, but he at least showed interest in meeting and talking. He had been a hit writer ("Bobbie Sue" for The Oak Ridge Boys and "Twenty Years Ago" for Kenny Rogers, to name a couple) and it takes some doing to get to write with people who have a great track record. Wood gained interest in writing with me when I shared with him that I had won an Emmy Award in the category of musical composer. After I showed him my winning song and video, I was "writing up," as they call it, which is when you get to do a co-write with someone with more accolades than you.

I had been working on a song called "Just Imagine," and because I was the new kid in town, it was my responsibility to bring an idea to the table. We spent the entire morning together, and before we broke for lunch, we had our song. Wood invited me to have lunch with him, and we became friends that day.

About a year later, I went to visit Wood to show him the book I had been writing that would feature our song in one of the chapters. I wanted to read the chapter to him and make sure he was comfortable including our co-write in my first book, *The Magic of a Song.* I read him the introduction, which talked about the song "I'd Like to Teach the World to Sing" and how that song had changed my life when I first heard it in a Coca-Cola commercial back when I was nine years old. As soon as I finished sharing the story with him, Wood looked at me and said, "Janie, do you realize that Roger Cook, who was one of the songwriters for that song, lives in Nashville? And by the way, he is a good friend of mine, and how would you like to have breakfast with him?" I had been imagining meeting people who were hit writers and famous artists, and here I was, getting to meet the songwriter who was probably the most instrumental person in igniting the spark in me to become a songwriter myself, as well as a guitar player and music teacher. Holy moly!

It All Depends on How Much You Allow Yourself to Imagine

That week, I got to have breakfast with Roger Cook, and he agreed to read my book and write me a quote for it. What are the odds? Talk about coming full circle. This is a good time to remind you that it all depends on how much you allow yourself to imagine.

Skip Franklin and Craig Duswalt are two of my favorite mentors, and one of their greatest sayings is, "Just keep showing up!" Craig says, "Always do your best in case someone is watching," and Skip tells me, "Always bring your guitar and look like a rock star." So I keep imagining, I always do my best in case someone is watching, and I keep showing up like a rock star! These are just a few of the blessings and miracles that have come my way since I took my big leap of faith.

With special thanks to Skip Franklin and Producer Matt Wilder:

- I got to co-write with John Carter Cash (Johnny and June's son), Wesley Orbison (Roy's son), and several other very talented writers at Johnny Cash's home in Nashville, Tennessee. (Our song is going on J. C. C.'s next album.)
- I got to sing at Willie Nelson's eightieth birthday party in Nashville, Tennessee, with John Carter Cash and Friends.
- I wrote and self-published my first book, *The Magic of a Song*.
- I recorded two CDs with some folks in Nashville who are not only some of the best session players on earth but also some of the kindest human beings in the universe.

- After having Faith Hill on my dream board, I ended up getting to record a duet I had written for my husband with her backup vocalist, Perry Coleman.
- The title song from my latest CD, *North Star* (inspired by Martha Beck), was voted number one in the Nashville Songwriter's Association International Top 40. (Thanks to everyone who voted!)

With special thanks to Craig Duswalt:

- I got to co-write the theme song for the California Women's Concert and perform it at the 2013 event in Long Beach, California.
- I got to be a special guest on Don Cromwell's (former Air Supply and Eddie Money bassist) radio show in LA.
- I got to speak and sing at Maryann Ehmann's "Create Your Magnificent Year" event in Coronado Bay, California, two years running.
- I got to speak and sing at Craig Duswalt's Rock-Star Marketing BootCamp and Personal Growth Weekend in LA.
- I got to record at Jimmy Jam's studio in LA.

**Imagination Brings Your Dreams to Life!
May You Listen Carefully to the Song in
Your Heart and Just Imagine!**

And now I'd like to introduce you to someone who has become an amazing friend and mentor, Skip Franklin. Skip has mentored many musicians in the country, and I was blessed to connect with him on my journeys in Nashville. I chose Skip to be my special guest author for the "Just Imagine" chapter because he has so wholeheartedly believed in my enthusiasm for using my imagination to bring my dreams to life.

Skip Franklin
Imagination has been one of the keys to my career. Initially, I used my imagination skills to develop my dreams and to "think bigger." As time went on, I began to use imagination in a more granular way—in developing the creative road map to get me there. It is crucial to visualize where you want to go. But don't stop there. Use that same creativity and imagination along the way. There will be roadblocks. There will be obstacles. There will be setbacks. Imagination and perseverance can help us navigate past those.

Many years ago, my software partners and I imagined a computer product that would use the award-winning works of *Far Side* cartoonist Gary Larson in a unique way. It was a very creative vision. But we didn't act on it. We thought, "Someone else is probably already doing this," or "Gary Larson wouldn't approve this type of product." In any event, we did not act. Two years later, there was still nothing on the market like our vision. And there was no *Far Side* product for computers. We decided to go for it. To take that "leap of faith." We spent a couple of months building a prototype of the product. I would cartoon some animation and then sleep while my partner took the animations and computerized them. My other partner worked on the product specs, and we all worked on our business proposal. We submitted it to Gary's agents, and after a cordial discussion on the phone, we got the door slammed in our faces. Absolute rejection.

Now it was time to use our imaginations to develop a "path" to get to Gary Larson himself. If we were to be rejected, we wanted to hear it from Gary himself. The full story is too long to recount here, but it was full of imagination. Our only guide was to make sure we were being *Far Side* enough—meaning that we were being weird enough for Gary. It took a couple of months to track down where Gary lived in Seattle, but eventually, we became fixtures in his neighborhood and recruited a couple of his neighbors to help us in our cause. Gary was recovering from surgery, so we felt a get-well package delivered to his back porch with our proposal would be most appropriate.

The final package to Gary involved a large African vase full of exotic plants that our "florist partner" had flown in from around the world. The University of Washington Entomology Lab donated a dozen exotic bugs that we carefully pinned to the plants, and then a professor shared with us recipes on how to best prepare each of these bugs for consumption. In our package we explained to Gary that the specimens were from our "edible bug collection." Our proposal was carefully placed underneath the vase, and on top was a get-well card that ended with, "Bon Appétit!" His neighbors had a key to Gary's gate, and they helped us place the African vase and proposal at his back door. And we waited. And waited.

Our imaginations (and our weirdness) intrigued Gary Larson, and he finally met with us. We had the product prototype already built, and we created a five-minute film showing groups of users enjoying, and laughing at, the cartoons and animations on the computer screen. Gary decided to partner with us instead of a couple of huge companies that had contacted him as well. The Amaze, Inc., *Far Side* Computer Calendar

& Screensaver went on to win product of the year for its category and became a bestseller in stores. The magic of imagination.

Fast-forward twenty years, and I was now in Nashville helping musical artists with their careers. The music industry requires the performing songwriters to use their imaginations not only in their songwriting craft but in their marketing strategies as well. I helped them on the business-strategy side, which usually incorporated a large dose of life-planning. The challenge is to find creative ways to reach your target market, to be uniquely yourself, and to somehow rise above the noise. It is important for these artists to visualize where they want to go. Really map it out in terms of building their brand, developing their core message, thinking of the letters they would like to receive from fans, and even creating a "calendar of events" for five years from now. What exactly does your imagined career look like? Work the details out.

One day, a mutual friend introduced me to an energetic songwriter from Alaska, and a few days later, I found myself at a Starbucks in Nashville having coffee with her. Janie Lidey was painting me a picture of her dream: what she wanted to do with her music, whom she wanted to reach, how she wanted to help them and, in turn, help change the world. Her inspiration and imagination were contagious.

Janie had recently transitioned out of her high school teaching job and was taking her "leap of faith" to follow her passion full time. She not only imagined her dream, she had the courage to take the leap. And being a songwriter, she had written a song called "Leap of Faith." I loved it!

Janie had already had several mountaintop moments in her career that fit nicely into her life vision. Now we just needed to imagine a path with more of those mountaintops. We had to develop an overriding theme and target market to help actualize the dream. And the fact that Janie is writing this book and that I am sharing this story is proof that the road map we imagined together was effective.

We concluded that Janie's number one life-theme was the fact she was already living many people's dream: to leave their safe job and pursue their passion full time. The fact that she was doing just that was inspiration enough. To many, she had already won. Perhaps the journey itself was a big part of the message here. Janie needed to chronicle her inspiring journey. And just as she was writing songs about her experiences, she should also be writing her books and developing her talks about her journey. And she did just that. Janie applied her wonderful imagination skills not only to her long-term vision, but also to all the magical footsteps along the way. She continues to bless others through her stories and lessons learned. Imagination in action!

Daily Habit Action Steps

- Think of something you would really like to see happen in your life, and then take your imaginary magic wand and go wild.

- Find time each and every day to live out your dream in your imagination.

- Act as if your dream has already come true and just imagine how it feels.

About the Song "Just Imagine"

This is the song I told you about that I got to co-write with Wood Newton. It seemed fitting to share it with you at the end of my "Just Imagine" chapter.

Just Imagine
Music & Lyrics by Janie Lidey & Wood Newton
Janie Lidey Publishing, BMI
Rope A Note Music, BMI
©2012

Einstein said we should use our imagination
And I remember how John Lennon said it too
Whatever you can dream of why not begin it now
Imagination makes your dreams come true

If you want peace to flow just like a river
If you want hope to float like a bird above the trees
If you want love to rain down from the heavens
Just imagine how it feels and let it be

What if you could live without your worries
And trouble didn't bother you anymore
And what if you could leave your past behind you
Unafraid of what tomorrow has in store

If you want peace to flow just like a river
If you want hope to float like a bird above the trees
If you want love to rain down from the heavens
Just imagine how it feels and let it be

You can fight against the current
Or ride the waves that rise and fall
As you're living your life story
Stop and read the writing on the wall

If you want peace to flow just like a river
If you want hope to float like a bird above the trees
If you want love to rain down from the heavens
Just imagine how it feels and let it be
Just imagine how it feels and let it be

Live in Gratitude

*Gratitude can transform common days into thanksgivings,
turn routine jobs into joy, and change ordinary
opportunities into blessings.*

~ William Arthur Ward ~

Do you know the power that gratitude holds in its ability to bring your dreams to life? Have you ever started your day by saying thank you—whether to God, the Universe, or whomever you feel like being grateful to—and then seen more blessings and miracles show up for you than usual? Do you have a system for living in gratitude? Do you have a system for helping raise gratitude in others? Do you spend time on a daily basis meditating, journaling, or praying?

This chapter is intended to help you gain insight into how you can not only raise your vibration by living in gratitude each day, but also how you can lift others up by sharing a bit of your gratitude with them.

Starting Your Day with Gratitude Will Help Lift You up and out of Bed in the Morning with a Brighter Disposition

Speaking words of gratitude before you even let your feet hit the floor in the morning will change the outcome of your day. I have developed the habit of setting my alarm for ten minutes earlier than I actually need to get up, hitting the snooze button, and then lying in bed thinking about all the things I have to be grateful for. Whether I am glad about something as simple as the fact that it is a sunny day or I am thankful for something as critical as having a medical test come back with good results, starting my day in gratitude helps lift me up and out of bed in the morning with a brighter disposition.

Once I hop up for the day, I open my journal and write three things I am grateful for. I like to follow that with three things I am going to be grateful for in the future (intentions) and then try to feel the gratitude flowing through me as if those things have already happened. This tends to raise my vibration yet a little higher.

Gratitude Journal Sample

I write a *G* for "Gratitude" at the top of my page, and then I write three things that I am grateful for.

Here is what that might look like:

G

- Today I am so grateful for the beautiful, sunny day we are going to have.
- Today I am so thankful that I have time to allow great ideas to flow through me for my new book.
- Today I am super excited and grateful for the new opportunities that keep flowing into my life.

Then I write a *D* for "Dreams," and I write three dreams I would like to see happen in my future. I write them as though they have already happened and I am feeling the gratitude I would feel in that moment.

D

- Today I am so grateful that I got a free upgrade to first class on my upcoming trip.
- Today I am grateful that money is flowing freely into my life so that I can do all the projects I am excited about doing to create positive change in the world.
- Today I am really thankful that my music has made its way to Faith Hill.

I am blown away at the events that occur in my life when I am diligent about my morning gratitude pages. It is amazing how new songs seem to just freely stream through me, money shows up seemingly out of the blue, I get bumped to first class for free, I get to record with Faith Hill's backup singer . . . As Glenn Morshower said in my Foreword, "We are shown time and time again that it is done unto us according to our faith. Does this mean that we get every little thing we wish for? Absolutely not! We are simply implementing **the law of thought equals outcome.** What we focus on increases exponentially."

Counting Your Blessings, No Matter Their Size, Usually Leads to Having More Blessings to Count

At times our own light goes out and is rekindled by a spark from another person. Each of us has cause to think with deep gratitude of those who have lighted the flame within us.

~ Albert Schweitzer ~

Lately, in my desire to quench my thirst for knowledge and understand gratitude on a deeper level, I am finding a lot of material that supports how being grateful on a daily basis helps bring the things we want most in life closer to us. What I would love to see more of is a message that supports how sharing our gratitude for others will also bless us more in our own lives, and in addition to that, it will raise the vibration in the people around us. The deeper I go on my journey with gratitude, the more I start to wonder about its power. What would happen if each of us were to commit to writing one note of gratitude to someone each day, no matter what? It only takes a moment to write a little note of thanks, and it can be either hand-delivered, mailed, or sent through one of the numerous social media outlets. What if people started acting more kindly because they received your note, and it raised them up a notch in their own walk with gratitude? You can write a note to a family member, a friend, a coworker, a store clerk, a teacher . . . the list is endless. What if we *acted as if* it were a global daily require-ment for every capable human being to write a note of thanks to someone else before the day's end? And what if we were to *begin it now* and then watch as a myriad of gratitude started showing up in the world? And what if we were to *dream big* and assume that in doing these daily notes of gratitude, we were chang-ing the vibration of love, peace, and happiness on our planet? And what if we threw our *just imagine* idea into the equation and required everyone to spend time each day thinking about a planet filled with grateful people?

Being Grateful—Not Just for What We Have Ourselves, but for What We Can Give to Others—Will Not Only Bless Us More in Our Own Lives, but It Will Also Raise the Vibration in the People around Us

When I applied for my job at East Anchorage High School in 1993, one of the questions the principal asked me was, "What is your philosophy on discipline?" He said he had heard that even my very large choir classes at the middle school where I taught didn't seem to have the typical discipline problems that tend to occur, especially with young teenagers. I, of course, answered with the more formal discipline policy I had in place, but then I told him the truth about why I really felt like kids were well behaved and respectful in my classes.

I had made a commitment to write a note of gratitude to at least one student a day. Even if I was busy, I would carve out a moment in my morning to jot a quick note to a kid and then hand it to them at some point during the class period. The note might say, "Just a little note to tell you how much I love having you in my class. Thanks for always showing up. Have a great day! Love Mrs. Lidey." Apparently, those kids that received a note started sharing its content with their classmates, because pretty soon it was evident that other kids were waiting for the day that they would get *their* note. Because they really wanted their own special note from Mrs. Lidey, they started showing up with enthusiasm-plus and shining their best light. And because I saw the positive effect it was having on so many kids, it made me feel so much more gratitude in my own day. I have run into so many students over the years that have told me they pinned my note of thanks on their wall and that it stayed there all the way through high school. Some still have that note tucked away in their wallet, purse, or drawer.

I have this theory that if one person can go out of their way to show compassion, then it will start a chain reaction of the same.

~ Rachel Joy Scott ~

And now I'd like to introduce you to a very special person in my life, Charlie Hewitt. Charlie is the CEO and president of Mirror Studios, Inc., and producer/ director at Fly Right Films. I chose Charlie to be my special guest author for the "Live in Gratitude" chapter because from the moment we met, the stories we have shared with one another have been all about the miracle of gratitude in our lives.

Charlie Hewitt

Gratitude Is the Antidote to Taking Things for Granted

I don't think much about fire. We have smoke detectors in every room and a family plan (meet in the front yard). Last week, though, I thought of little else. During the hottest week on record, a wildfire was raging out of control near our home. When the winds shifted and smoke filled the neighborhood, we packed a bag, shoved photo albums in a box, and watched a lot of online news as three hundred firefighters battled the blaze in steep, dangerous terrain. Hundreds of people were poised to evacuate. The weather forecast promised rain, but also high winds. Our prayers were answered when the rain arrived first. When a sprinkle turned into a steady downpour, the sense of relief was palpable throughout the community. We've all experienced that wave of gratitude when a dreaded danger passes: the biopsy results come back negative; your teen walks through the door, hours late but unscathed; you slam on the brakes and you come to a stop inches from the car in front of you. For a few minutes or a few days, we have a heightened sense of gratitude. We *notice* the color of the flowers, the sound of the birds, the flavor of our food. Then, all too soon, that awareness of what is quietly going *right* is replaced by the persistent clanging of what is going *wrong*:

"This coffee is cold"; "My knee is stiff"; "This house is a mess."

One of my greatest blessings has been the realization that those waves of gratitude are not just available when something awful doesn't happen. They are available to us every day.

Something magical happens when we take the time to look around and begin to **feel** grateful. That's when the universe begins to take notice.

An attitude of gratitude is something that is cultivated. There is something to be grateful for everywhere you look. Here is a simple exercise: Write down one hundred things you're grateful for. The first dozen or so will come easily: children, health, family, spouse, job, car, food, and so on, but a subtle shift begins to take place when you get a little further down the list. You begin to write down the things you can't see, the things you can't touch. And then your list explodes. It's everywhere. You begin to be mindful and start to pay attention to the things around you that we all take for granted. The smell of fresh-cut grass, the sound of the birds singing in the morning, the tiny noises a newborn infant makes, the ability to take a deep breath, a soft bed, shoes, arriving safely at your destination— whether it is touching down at an airport or at the bottom of a flight of stairs.

When you concentrate on thankfulness, you begin to feel it. Notice what happens to your body. How does it make *you* feel? My respiration changes, and I feel a flutter in my stomach. I feel alive—both calmed and energized at the same time. And when you are busy counting your blessings, you have much less time to count your sorrows.

An old friend of mine recently and very unexpectedly lost the love of his life, his wife of thirty years, to a heart attack. When I heard the news I sent him a note right away expressing my sympathy. His reply humbled me: "I am so grateful that I had thirty spectacular years with her. She's in heaven now, and I will be able to see her again." Of course he is devastated by the loss of his wife, and there will be many grief-filled days to come, but he has chosen to start this journey with gratitude. His sense of gratitude for thirty spectacular years makes all the difference in the way he's dealing with his loss.

I believe that gratitude is a gift offered to all of us. When we choose to accept that gift, we begin to see the world through a more beautiful lens. Gratitude is a mind-set—a habit, if you will—that comes from being mindful and noticing the bounty we have all around us.

Daily Habit Action Steps

- Set your alarm for ten minutes earlier than you need to get up and just rest in gratitude for those ten minutes.

- Buy yourself a new journal and spend ten minutes in the morning writing the three things you're grateful for, followed by your three dreams, and then **feel** those dreams as though they have already come true.

- Choose at least one person each day to say thank you to.

- Choose at least one person each day to write a note of thanks to and either hand-deliver it, mail it, or use social media to get it to them.

About the Song "Thank You"

The inspiration behind this song came from my amazing friend Stephanie Adriana Westover. She mentioned one day that it would be so perfect if I were to write a "Thank You" song, because gratitude is so big in the world right now and it is so much a part of how we each live our lives. The night before she told me that, I literally was dreaming about a "Thank You" song I sang back in college and then later taught to my choirs. It seemed like a sign, and soon after, this song came along.

Thank You
Inspired by Stephanie Adriana Westover
Music & Lyrics by Janie Lidey, BMI
©2016

T H A N K   Y O U   —   T H A N K   Y O U

If you say these two words before you
even put your feet on the floor
You will wake up on the right side
of your bed like never before
And if you say these two words before you
close your eyes and turn out the light
You will wake up in the morning feeling
like you grew a set of wings overnight

Thank you for a good night's sleep
Thank you for the air I breathe
Thank you for the morning sun
Thank you for a day of fun

My feet don't even touch the ground for the day
Until I take the time to say

T H A N K   Y O U   —   T H A N K   Y O U

Leap of Faith

When I lay me down to sleep for the night
I say a prayer in thanks for everything
that's going so right
And then I dream of all the possibilities
That I know tomorrow tomorrow holds for me

Thank you for a good night's sleep
Thank you for the air I breathe
Thank you for the morning sun
Thank you for a day of fun

My feet don't even touch the ground for the day
Until I take the time to say

T H A N K   Y O U   —   T H A N K   Y O U

Thank you for a good night's sleep
Thank you for the air I breathe
Thank you for the morning sun
Thank you for a day of fun

Let the Music Lift You

Music is the electrical soil in which the spirit lives, thinks and invents.

~ Ludwig van Beethoven ~

How much of a role does music play in your life? Do you listen to your favorite songs first thing in the morning? Do you use music in your meditations? Do you turn on your favorite station when you're driving in your car? Do you prefer to read, write, or study in silence or with your favorite music playing in the background? Do you crank up your stereo while doing your dishes or laundry?

This chapter is intended to help you gain insight into how music can truly lift you up, rock your world, raise your vibration, heighten your senses, and help you power up your leap.

You Can Truly Raise Your Vibration
through the Magic of a Song

Every time I hear the song "Close to You" by Karen Carpenter, I am transported to my back porch in Bedford, Massachusetts. The song is coming from my little blue transistor radio, and I am lying out in the sun with my big sister Kris. She is wearing her orange bikini, and I am in my little yellow bikini. I am six or seven years old, and I can smell the fresh summer air and the chlorine from the pool. I can taste the chip and dip that Mum has set out for us. I am basking in the greatness of how much I love getting to spend time with my teenaged sister. Every time I hear that song, I can **feel** all these feelings as though they were really happening right here and now. Music has the power to make you see, smell, taste, and feel. You can truly raise your vibration through the magic of a song.

A few years ago, my dad was diagnosed with Alzheimer's and ALS. He was in his eighties when we first started noticing a decline in his awareness, his speech, and his ability to remember certain parts of his past. As his memory faded, I became aware of the power that music held in igniting parts of his brain that were otherwise just gone.

While visiting my parents one spring morning, my dad looked down at my guitar and said, "I didn't know you played the guitar." Hearing those words that day almost made something inside of me die. You see, when I was twelve years old, my dad bought me my first guitar. I started writing songs soon after, and every time I wrote something new, Mum and Dad would sit in the kitchen with me and listen to me play those new songs. My parents came to all my talent shows and concerts, and then when I asked my dad if I could go away to a music college, he answered with a resounding "Yes!" I remember having friends whose parents told them they could minor in music, but they had to major in something more practical so they would have something to fall back on. Not my dad! He was always supportive of my music and listened willingly and enthusiastically through the years.

Instead of letting my dad's words that day strip me to the core, I just reached down and grabbed my guitar out of its case and said, "I don't know, Dad, I think you gave me my first guitar when I was twelve." I then began to play some of the old songs that I had played for my dad over the years, and it was as though the vibration of the music opened a portal that had otherwise been closed in his brain. I think that because the music made him **feel** something, the very act of feeling brought back some of his memory. Suddenly, Dad started communicating with me in a more lucid manner, his speech became more articulate, and it was as though the music brought him back to me in that moment.

Music cleanses the understanding; inspires it, and lifts it into a realm which it would not reach if it were left to itself.

~ Henry Ward Beecher ~

On May 10, 2016, Dad got his promotion to Heaven. The love of his life and all of his children were there to help him kick off his journey, and with my guitar in hand, Mum, Kris, Bill, Susie, Carol, and I sang Dad to Heaven. And even though our dad was on morphine and seemed to have one foot in Heaven already, his toes were still tapping to the beat of the music.

The longer I live this life out, the more I discover the many ways in which music enhances even the most mundane activities. Here are a few thoughts on how you can *let the music lift you.*

Music for Your Chores
One day I was doing my dishes and laundry, and as I passed by my television, I reached out and flipped on the '70s music channel. Why I didn't realize this long

ago, I'll never know, but suddenly I was dancing my way from the sink in the kitchen and feeling all happy and peppy as I made my way down the hall to my laundry room. And now I only do my chores with the stereo cranked.

Life seems to go on without effort when I am filled with music.
~ George Eliot ~

Music on the Road

Road trips, whether short or long, are always more enjoyable when listening to your favorite songs. I love the latest testimonial I received about my new CD, *North Star*. It came from a couple that commutes to and from Los Angeles every day, and they said, "We just keep your CD in the car at all times and now our commute is so peaceful. We can't possibly have road rage when listening to your songs."

On some nights I still believe that a car with the gas needle on empty can run about fifty more miles if you have the right music very loud on the radio.
~ Hunter S. Thompson ~

Music for Your Workout

I love to cross-country ski, and I am lucky to live right next to some of the finest Nordic ski trails in the world. When I am gliding through the gently lit woods on a snowy night, I feel like I am living in a snow globe. And don't most snow globes have a little switch on the bottom that you can wind up and hear a special song playing while watching the snowflakes fall inside your globe? Several years ago, I realized that I was counting the minutes as I did my hour-long workout on the ski loop. So I decided to bring my ear buds the next time and crank up my favorite Pink Floyd album, *Dark Side of the Moon,* and I ended up going the extra mile and looping around a second time.

Music gives a soul to the universe, wings to the mind, flight to the imagination and life to everything.
~ Plato ~

And now I'd like to introduce you to my friend Don Cromwell. I met Don when our mutual friend Craig Duswalt asked him to have me as a guest on his radio show, DC Live. Don is a producer, songwriter, and musician based in Los Angeles who toured as the bass player with the renowned pop group Air Supply in the '80s and then played bass with rock legend Eddie

Money for six years. I chose Don to be my special guest author for the "Let the Music Lift You" chapter because he has years and years of firsthand experience in the power of music to lift you up.

Don Cromwell

As the eyes are the windows to our souls, music is the lift in our spirits. Emotions strong and pure, raw and simple are captured through lyrics that touch us and melodies that move us. Throughout history, music has been a constant source of creative and listening pleasure. From the magnificent classical composers of yesteryear to thundering concertos and storytelling operas, through jazz, pop, rock, country, punk, ethnic, rap, and hip-hop, there are sounds, styles, and moods that will accompany each and every one of us on our personal journey through life, if we, like the Doobie Brothers tell us in song, just "listen to the music."

For me as a youngster, the fifth of ten children living in Novato, California, while my dad was stationed at Hamilton Air Force Base, I had to wait my turn to get ahold of the small, gray portable record player we shared among us. To this day, I can recall sitting on the living room floor listening to 45-rpm records of "The Ballad of the Green Berets" by Barry Sadler, "The Lonely Bull" by the Tijuana Brass, "Eve of Destruction" by Barry McGuire, "Exodus" by Ferrante and Teicher, and of course, "Johnny Angel" by Shelley Fabares. Boy, did I have a crush on her—and I was sure she really meant to sing "Donny Angel." My sisters would listen to Elvis Presley, of course, and how could I forget Ricky Nelson—I don't think my sister Chris ever did . . .

My dad retired from the air force and took a job with the Federal Aviation Agency at Oakland Airport. After a year of stressful commuting, he moved the family to San Leandro, a blue-collar city within close proximity to his work. Even at my young age, it turned out to be a life-changing event for me, because the sixth grade class at St. Felicitas Catholic School had no room for me, and for the first time, I would now be attending public school. All I can say is "What a difference!" Kids were going steady; the girls were wearing their guys' sweaters, playing spin the bottle, and making out; and the music was always playing. Hey, it was all new to this boy, and I must admit, I didn't mind it one bit!

I'll save more details of my personal life for a book I might write someday, but this is all relevant because it was at my new neighbor's house across the street that the effect of music in my life was taken to another level. Soon after my family moved into the new house on Sullivan Avenue, my neighbor Warren and I were in the lower level of their home (all the houses on the street have the same floor plan, and we called them basements, but they were really just the bottom floor), listening to records at random, when he played songs by a group from England that I had never heard of. Yep, you may have guessed it: The Beatles. The first song was "I Wanna Hold Your Hand," followed by "Please Please Me," and if I recall correctly, "Love Me Do." I went crazy with the vibrant sound, the uplifting feeling, the words, the melodies—it all hit me right between the eyes and like a laser to the heart. I loved what I was hearing and wanted to be a musician right then and there; I'd had no previous desire to play an instrument, had never given a remote thought to any such endeavor. But I picked up a tennis racket, held it like a guitar, and played along. I knew I was hooked.

Not long after this epiphany, my two best friends, Bill and Russ, both got guitars and started lessons. Russ had a nice Gibson, Bill a red Fender Mustang. Before long, they were playing "Pipeline" and "Wipe Out," and I was jealous. Darn it, I needed a guitar! Being from a family of ten children, my dad wasn't about to buy me a guitar, and I had no problem with that; he was a great provider, and we never wanted for anything. So I saved up enough money from allowance and odd jobs and bought an Airline guitar from Montgomery Ward. My sister Chris worked there and got me a discount; I believe the price was twenty-two dollars out the door. Another clear memory I have is of me riding home on my bicycle, holding the cardboard box under my right arm, trying desperately not to drop it . . . I was on my way!

That was the official start of my journey as a musician, both amateur and professional. I switched to bass guitar as my main instrument in my sophomore year of high school when the lead singer in our band couldn't sing "Light My Fire" by the Doors and play the bass part at the same time (it was pretty tricky). We simply switched equipment and never switched back. A lot has gone on since those days, far too much to get into here, but suffice it to say that over the years, I've ridden the roller coaster that is the music business: the highest of highs, the lowest of lows, and everything in between. I've played in front of four drunks in Kodiak, Alaska, at 3 a.m., as well as sixteen thousand fans at two back-to-back sold-out shows at the Budokan in Tokyo. I've played in countless nightclub bands, reselling music gear bought through the Recycler Classifieds newspaper ads (way, way before Craigslist or eBay) to help pay the rent. All the great friends and musicians along the way, the laughs and the heartaches, a fantastic five-year run with Air Supply followed by several great years with Eddie Money—all of these things were a part of my personal journey, and I wouldn't trade them for the world.

Throughout it all—for me, at least—along with faith and family, music has been the stabilizer in my life and the lift in my spirit. I still wake up every day with a song in my heart, a dream in my head, and a feeling that the best is yet to come. The power of music is just that: power. It can soothe an aching soul, comfort a saddened heart, bring back a cherished memory, or challenge a competitive spirit. Music is a gift to us all and a gift to be shared. There is a message to be heard and a mood that will inspire. We must open up our hearts and ears to feel that power and, as Janie says, get the lift that will power up your own personal leap of faith. In the end, I simply try to follow the sentiment of some of my own lyrics; in this "Crazy Kind of Life," where we strive for peace in our lives and in our hearts, while we pursue our dreams and follow our passions, never forget to "Take Time" and enjoy life!

Daily Habit Action Steps

• Always do your chores to music. You will be amazed at how much fun you will have, and you may even find yourself dancing from your kitchen to your laundry room.

• Have a good sound system in your car and stock up on different kinds of music for different kinds of driving. If you need to calm your road rage, choose songs that are peaceful. If you need to stay awake at the wheel, choose songs that are up-tempo and have a driving force behind them.

• Go through your music collection and make yourself a special soundtrack for your workouts.

• Play music every day. It stimulates your brain and usually inspires your heart in some way.

About the Song "Go The Extra Mile"
Glenn Morshower had just finished speaking at Craig Duswalt's Personal Growth Weekend in LA, during which he shared this incredibly descriptive line: "Base the notes you choose to play upon the song you want to hear." As soon as I heard those words, I could feel a song welling up inside of me. His program The Extra Mile played right into the song, and that is where the title came from.

Go The Extra Mile
Inspired by Glenn Morshower
Music & Lyrics by Janie Lidey, BMI
©2016

Have your arms wide open
Choose to stand and allow
Celebrate this moment that is right
here that is right now

You are the new day
You awake a brand new child
You can choose the road less
travelled go the extra mile

Allow yourself to dance away your fear
Love the one you see within your mirror
Base the notes you choose to play
upon the song you want to hear

You are the one who gets to write your script for you
You get to choose the road you drive
Every moment is as good as you decide it to be
Enjoy your climb

You are the new day
You awake a brand new child
You can choose the road less
travelled go the extra mile

Allow yourself to dance away your fear
Love the one you see within your mirror
Base the notes you choose to play
upon the song you want to hear

Allow yourself to dance away your fear
Love the one you see within your mirror
Base the notes you choose to play
upon the song you want to hear
Go the extra mile . . . Go the extra mile . . .

Laugh while You Leap

At the height of laughter, the universe is flung into a kaleidoscope of new possibilities.

~ Jean Houston ~

Do ever find yourself in need of a good dose of laughter after taking a big, bold leap of faith? Do you have any sure and ready methods for getting the laughter started?

Sometimes when you leap, you end up soaring like an eagle and other times you fall quickly and painfully to the hard, cold ground below. While there, you have to decide whether you're going to laugh, cry, or laugh while you're crying.

It's not what happens to you, but how you react to it that matters.

~ Epictetus ~

This chapter is intended to help you gain insight into how you can choose to include laughter in your daily routine and how it can lift you up and help you with your daily leaps of faith.

If you really think about the times in your life when you have laughed the hardest, you will probably remember that during that laughter you were at your best. You felt less tense. It made you feel super happy. It really connected you to the person you were laughing with. If you weren't feeling well when you started laughing, you felt much better when you were finished. And if any pictures were taken at that time, you probably found that you looked more beautiful while laughing.

There Are Certain People in Our Lives That Make Us Laugh More than Any Others, and It Is Important to Find a Way to Stay Connected with Those People

When I moved to Alaska, I left my whole family behind in California. I have three sisters and a brother, and we grew up very close. One of the things that I began to notice after being away from my family was that I never laughed as hard with anyone else as I did with them. And without that laughter in my life, I began to feel a bit deflated. I realized that there are certain people in our lives that make us laugh more than any others, and it is important to find a way to stay connected with those people.

Sometimes You Can't Be with the Ones Who Make You Laugh the Most, but You Can Always Pick up the Phone and Call Them

The only way I could really stay connected with my family after my big move to Alaska was to talk with them on the telephone. One day, I was talking with my little sister Carol, and the phone call ended in the kind of laughter that leaves you in tears. Our phone calls always consisted of the good and the bad things happening in our lives, and then we would end our conversation with "But thank God we have our health!" Well this time, our call was filled with conversations about fear and doubt and about the fact that we were both experiencing some major health issues. Carol had a heart condition and had to have open-heart surgery to repair a hole that had been increasing in size since birth. And I had a gaping hole in my head after leaping into a steep mogul field and putting a ski through my skull, leaving me with a depressed skull fracture and a torn durra. Before the doctors realized the seriousness of the injury, they just sewed me back up and sent me home. Over the course of that week, I was leaking cerebral fluid (which can't be replaced the way blood can be, so if I seem a little dingy at times, I have an excuse), and by week's end, I was in the operating room having cranial surgery to take out the broken bone fragments, sew up the durra, and get an IV of antibiotics going to kill the infection that the doctor said was sending me on my way to meningitis. At the end of our call, Carol and I said our usual "But thank God we have our health," and then we realized, "Oh my God, no we don't!" We then proceeded to laugh until we cried. Somehow, no matter how bad the stories have gotten over the years, we have managed to find our way back to laughter. And every time we do, it lifts us back onto our feet and preps us for another leap of faith.

Always Find Your Way Back to Laughter

Laughter can come from so many sources. You can laugh by talking to your favorite funny person on the phone, by watching a funny TV show or movie, by reading the funnies, by going to a live comedy show, by playing with or watching animals . . . the list goes on.

Many of you have probably heard the story of a man named Norman Cousins. Norman was a professor of medical humanities for the School of Medicine at the University of California, Los Angeles. He did research on the biochemistry of human emotions, which he believed were the key to human beings' success in fighting illness. Norman actually spent many hours watching videos of the television show *Candid Camera* and various comic films to accelerate his recovery from a crippling illness. He truly believed in the power of laughter to cure disease.

We are all survivors of something in this life. The path that leads us to the most happiness, the highest financial well-being, and the healthiest minds and bodies is full of ups and downs. And while it takes a huge amount of courage and imagination to leap, and sometimes struggle accompanies your path, it's so important to laugh while you're crying. You will be amazed at how it lifts you up.

And now I would like to introduce you to one of my favorite people on the planet, my little sister Carol Casas. Carol is a top-selling realtor in the Silicon Valley, and I chose her to be my special guest author for the "Laugh while You Leap" chapter because she inspires me to laugh every single day, no matter what I may be going through.

Carol Casas
As much as I truly believe I have had a rich and wonderful life, if you look at the major health events I have

endured, both personally and within my family, one may think otherwise. Heart surgery at age twenty-two, my husband being diagnosed with cancer when I was thirty-two, my daughter being diagnosed with melanoma when I was forty-six, and then this past year, at age fifty-two, I again had to have two heart procedures to gain back my own health. I sure could make a case for being down and out, and with my story, people around me would buy it. But I know that life is filled with ups and downs, and these experiences, although difficult, have made me the human being I am today. Enduring these tough life moments in the past has made me so grateful for the future. I have laughed through it, cried through it, and laughed while I cried.

Prior to my heart surgery thirty years ago, my doctor gave me a booklet about how laughter helps to heal. During the surgery, they had opened up my chest cavity to repair an atrial septal defect that I had since birth. It was an excruciating recovery for sure. Coughing, sneezing, lifting, and sleeping were all pretty darn hard. But since I had read in that booklet that laughter was a great recovery tool, I laughed with my mom and dad and my sister Sue as much as possible. It was painful, but it also made me feel alive. I had made it through major surgery, and I was celebrating life! I was very sore for many weeks from all that laughter so, one day, I picked up that booklet I had read about laughter being good for recovery to see if there were any other pearls of wisdom to get well sooner. I didn't learn much more, but I had my own little giggling party after rereading and realizing it actually said that laughter is great for *family members*, not the patient, to get through the scariness of a loved one in pain. My entire family gets a good chuckle even today thinking about my misinterpreting the recovery materials. However, I may have misread it the first time, but I am convinced that the laughter, even though I was sometimes crying in pain while I laughed, helped me heal just as much as it did those loved ones around me.

It really is all in the way you deal with the challenges that life throws you. Whether it is a major event or one of those tiny moments during the day that may make you sad, tense, or hurt, laughter will undoubtedly help. In the midst of my own health issues in 2016, I was managing the care for my aging parents and more specifically dealing with the daily challenges of my dad's declining health due to Alzheimer's and ALS. I thank God for my three sisters, my brother, and my mother through all this because humor truly brought us through it. Mom dealt with daily caregiving and all us kids lent daily support to my mom, made monthly plane trips to their assisted-living community, took care of their finances, and tried to stay ahead of their levels of needed care. It was exhausting, but the glue that kept us together was laughter. We have always been a silly family, and to this day, when we are together, at least one us collapses in a fit of laughter hourly. We have to thank our parents for this, as they always found humor in the toughest of situations. We have now passed this wonderful trait down to our children and grandchildren. There is nothing better than listening to a toddler's belly laugh. It will make your day every time.

In May 2016, my dad passed away. It was sad and painful, but a blessing as well. Our family of seven spent three glorious days together talking, singing, crying, reminiscing, joking, and yes, laughing. Dad was still a bit alert during those final days, and it seemed the more we laughed around him, the more at peace he was and the calmer we became. Of course losing a parent is hard, but what better way to honor them than to talk about all the great memories. In our family, most of those memories involved laughter. So we carried on our goofiness for those precious days, got scolded by the staff for being too loud and silly, and we loved every minute of it. As my dad took his final breaths, we cried, and then we cried some more. But then, in our usual Sykes Family fashion, we laughed through the tears and cried through the laughter. We all knew this moment in life would be one of the saddest, but we also knew that leaping forward with laughter while we were crying was the start of our journey toward healing from our grief.

Daily Habit Action Steps

- Decide that you are going to laugh as part of your daily mental-health workout.

- If you find yourself crying about something, see if you can turn it into laughter. The energy is very similar, but one usually leaves you feeling much better than the other.

- Call that person in your life that makes you laugh more than any other.

- Play with your pet more, and if you don't have your own, go to the local zoo. Animals do the funniest things.

- Look up all the funny movies you'd like to watch or rewatch. Keep the list handy so that when you are in need of a good laugh, you can readily pick one out to watch.

About the Song "Laugh While You're Cryin'"
Standing in the shower one morning in 2006, this song had its beginning. It came to me after thinking about my conversations with my little sister Carol over the years and how even in the worst of times, we have managed to laugh while we're cryin'.

Laugh While You're Cryin'
Inspired by Carol Casas
Music & Lyrics by Janie Lidey, BMI
©2007

Did you ever feel cold standing in a hot shower
Smell somethin' foul while you're breathin' in a flower
And did you ever have a day where you
feel like nothin's goin' your way
Every time you turn around somethin' isn't okay

You can laugh while you're cryin'
live while you're dyin'
Smile when you're mad be happy when you're sad
It all comes down to livin' in the moment
and lovin' what you're doin'
Even when you don't

Have you ever been lost even though
you just found your way
Or been in love and had the guy just toss you away
And have you ever been late even though you left early
Had to be on task when you were feelin' kinda squirly

You can laugh while you're cryin'
live while you're dyin'
Smile when you're mad be happy when you're sad

116

It all comes down to livin' in the moment
and lovin' what you're doin'
Even when you don't

I wanna laugh
And I wanna live
And I wanna smile and be happy for a little while

You can laugh while you're cryin'
live while you're dyin'
Smile when you're mad be happy when you're sad
It all comes down to livin' in the moment
and lovin' what you're doin'
Even when you don't

You can laugh while you're cryin'
live while you're dyin'
Smile when you're mad be happy when you're sad
It all comes down to livin' in the moment
and lovin' what you're doin'
Even when you don't

Leap with Love

The notion of developing unconditional compassion is daunting. Most people, including myself, must struggle even to reach the point where putting others' interests on a par with our own becomes easy. We should not allow this to put us off, however. And while undoubtedly there will be obstacles on the way to developing a genuinely warm heart, there is the deep consolation of knowing that in doing so we are creating the conditions for our own happiness. The more we truly desire to benefit others, the greater the strength and confidence we develop and the greater the peace and happiness we experience. Through love, through kindness, through compassion we establish understanding between ourselves, and others. This is how we forge unity and harmony.

~ Dalai Lama ~

Is your leap fueled by fear or love? Do you make decisions based solely on your needs and wants, or do you choose your path according to how you might benefit others?

This chapter is intended to give you insight into how love can truly power up your leap. I leave you with some quotes, stories, and finally a song that is meant to raise your vibration and help inspire you to *leap with love.*

Looking back over all the leaps of faith I have taken in my life, I realize that the greatest leaps of all were the ones taken with love. No matter how big or small, when love is at the wheel and fear is thrown to the curb, blessings and miracles always seem to appear. Now more than ever, we need to dig deep and choose love over fear. Both are contagious, and we all have the power within to be love, share love and spread the ease of love. We live in a world filled with disease, and love takes the "dis" out of "disease."

The Greatest Leaps of All Are the Ones Taken with Love

In Habit #2, I shared with you the story about my husband going out and buying me the painting of the mountain goat leaping from one sheer cliff to another with the word "FAITH" as the caption. Sean chose love over fear and took a huge leap of faith when he hopped aboard my dream. His love for me, and the encouragement that came with that beautiful gift, helped me lose my fear and leap with a greater faith than ever before.

In this final chapter, I want to share two stories with you. The first is a story I will simply call "Sam's Story." It is about a leap of faith I took out of pure, unconditional love for someone and how it not only helped that person live *their* best life but altered how I have lived mine. The second is a story I will simply call "My Starfish Story." It is about making a difference, one act of love at a time.

Sam's Story

While teaching at East High School, I had the responsibility of auditioning students between the ages of fourteen and eighteen for the East High swing choir. This was the top performance group in the choir program at East, and with only twenty-four spots to fill (many of which were already occupied by kids that were grandfathered in from the previous years), it was a very emotional time of year for both the students and myself. There might be fifty kids that tried out and only seven or eight slots open.

One year, I had a student trying out that I will just call Sam. Sam was in the men's choir and the concert choir but had not made it into the swing choir yet. He was going into his senior year, and with only a few requirements left to graduate, he had room in his schedule to be in men's choir, concert choir, *and* swing choir. Sam was a good singer with a pretty decent work ethic and enthusiasm-plus when it came to singing, but there was just one little problem. Sam was a little bit "pitchy." To those of you who aren't musically inclined, that means that sometimes he sang a little off-key.

When the auditions were over, I had my work cut out for me. I had to decide whether to make my decisions based on my own ego and the level of excellence the choir could achieve or on the love I felt for my students and what would be the best choice based on the needs of each individual human being. There was a student who tried out for the same voice part as Sam who was younger and a little less focused but had a great sense of pitch and would create a better blend in the choir. If I chose him, the choir would be more solid and I knew that the remaining students in the group would be happier. So did I take him or did I take Sam, whom I would have to work extra hard with to get his voice to blend in with the group? I knew that if Sam made it into the swing choir that year, it would be something that would enhance his life beyond what most people might imagine.

Sam had a pretty tough go of it in his home life, as he had a mom who was very ill. He took care of her almost every night, and coming to school each day and being involved with music was the highlight of his life. If I placed him on the swing choir roster, I would have the other swing choir members to recon with because I knew that they would challenge why I had taken Sam over the other kid with better pitch. But I was the adult here, the one who had a vision far greater than that of just letting the better voice in. It was about the whole human being.

It was about what this could mean in a kid's life. It was about loving without condition. I chose to *leap with love* and allow Sam the opportunity to shine his light and live his best life during that last year of high school.

Sam's senior year might have just been the best year of his life. He came to the choir room three times a day and usually spent the lunch hour in the music wing as well. He got to shine his light as a member of the swing choir and even got to sing a solo here and there. Sam also loved to dance, and during his senior year, we got a special invitation to perform with a group out of Africa called Sharon Katz and the Peace Train. We got to sing and dance on the largest stage in the city in front of thousands of people, and although Sam may not have been the best singer in the group, he just might have been the best dancer. I will never forget the joy I felt watching him let his light shine on that stage.

This story could just be an ordinary story with a happy ending, but what it turned out to be was an extraordinary story with a happy ending—to Sam's life. During the fall of the year after Sam graduated, he came to the choir room to visit. He was, as usual, singing and dancing his way around the music wing. He was so jolly, and his smile was born of a deep and undying enthusiasm for music. Being a member of the East High swing choir in his senior year had empowered Sam beyond what most people could know.

One week later, I got the news that Sam had passed away in his sleep. There was no explanation for his sudden death other than that it was believed to be of natural causes.

Had I let my fear cause me to choose differently that previous year, Sam would have missed all the amazing experiences he was blessed with. Fear of picking the wrong student for the choir, fear of having the other swing choir members question my decision-making skills, fear of letting the younger student down, fear of having a less than perfect choir, fear of having to spend a lot of extra time working with a student that needed some extra coaching . . . the list goes on. For some reason, and I believe it had to do with the combination of God's favor on Sam's life as well as His desire to enlighten me more about unconditional love, I chose Sam.

When You Leap with Love, Blessings and Miracles Appear

One individual who lives and vibrates to the energy of pure love and reverence for all of life will counterbalance the negativity of 750,000 individuals who calibrate at the lower weakening levels.

~ Dr. Wayne Dyer ~

My Starfish Story

Several years ago, I was invited to do a house concert at an old friend's home in the Bay Area of California. It would take place in the little town of Mountain View, and my host thought there would be anywhere from twenty to thirty guests in attendance. I was going to be in the area for a few other events anyway, so it was easy for me to put it on my calendar. It would be a great opportunity to reconnect with some special friends from my past, make some new friends, and hopefully raise a few more people's vibration with the songs and stories from my new album and book, *The Magic of a Song.*

On the night before the concert, I got a phone call from my old friend saying that things hadn't exactly turned out the way she planned. There were only going to be six people at the performance, and two of them were her own children. She said that considering the circumstances, she would totally understand if I wanted to cancel. Suddenly that inner voice was back in my head saying things like "Oh great, now you are only going to make one hundred bucks for the night, and with only a few people in the house, you'll be lucky if you sell a few CDs and books! You might as well just take your friend up on her offer and cancel."

After putting that inner voice in its place, I realized that it didn't matter to me if there was going to be one person in attendance or a crowd of one million. If something I was going to share in a story or a song that evening had the potential to raise the vibration in even one person's life, my purpose as an entertainer on this planet that day would be fulfilled. I chose to leap with love, bring my guitar and show up like a rock star, and do my best in case someone was watching. (Remember those wise words from my mentors Skip Franklin and Craig Duswalt in Habit #4?)

I showed up for my house concert in Mountain View ready to rock 'n' roll. My sister Carol was my chauffeur and helped me carry my little PA system in and get everything set up. I could have gone acoustic with such a small crowd, but I still wanted to share the full scope of the performance I had planned for the bigger audience. To do so, I needed my sound system and computer to play some of my backup tracks for a few of the songs I had recently recorded in Nashville. I had the blessing of working with some of the most amazing session players while recording *The Magic of a Song* and wanted to make this a really special show, regardless of the size of my audience.

My host had set up a beautiful area in her home for me to perform in. She was a singer herself and had a little stage area set up in her family room where she and her band would practice together. So Carol and I went to work and set up as though we would have a room full of people. As with most of the house concerts I do, we did a meet and greet over cocktails and hors d'oeuvres and then gathered in the family room for an intimate evening of stories and songs. I could tell that there was a little bit of discomfort on the guests part seeing that I had come all the way from Alaska, had set up such a nice stage area, had CDs and books for sale . . . and here we were, in an almost-empty room.

What happened after sharing my first few stories and songs was **amazing**. One of the guests stood up and with great intensity said, "I don't mean to be rude or anything, but can you please stop the concert for a little while? I am going to go out into our neighborhood and invite people over. This is just too dang good for anyone to miss!" You can only imagine how that made me feel! Of course I agreed, and we extended the cocktail hour while this kind gentleman attempted to fill the room at my smallest-ever house concert.

The magical connection that we as entertainers make with our audience is something that can literally change a life in one heartfelt moment. I'll never forget the lady who came rushing up to talk with me and said that she used to be a painter but hadn't picked up her brushes in years. After hearing my "Leap of Faith" song and listening to my story about retiring early from a successful teaching career to become a full-time singer-songwriter, artist, author, and speaker, she decided she was going to go home, break out her brushes, and become an artist again. When you leap with love, you just never know what kind of impact you might have on one person's special life.

That little house concert at my old friend's home turned out to be one of my favorite events of the year. After a few more guests were reeled in from the neighborhood, I took up from where I had left off (actually, I repeated the first two stories and songs because no one wanted the new guests to miss out), and we had an amazing, intimate evening filled with stories, songs, and a shift in the vibration in each of us in the room, including my own.

You Just Never Know What Kind of Impact You Might Have on One Person's Special Life

The Starfish Story
An anonymous story that ties in so perfectly here—I just had to share it!

A young man is walking along the ocean and sees a beach on which thousands and thousands of starfish have washed ashore. Farther along, he sees an old man, walking slowly and stooping often, picking up one starfish after another and tossing each one gently into the ocean.

"Why are you throwing starfish into the ocean?" the young man asks.

"Because the sun is up and the tide is going out, and if I don't throw them farther in, they will die."

"But, old man, don't you realize there are miles and miles of beach and starfish all along it? You can't possibly save them all! You can't even save one-tenth of them. In fact, even if you work all day, your efforts won't make any difference at all."

The old man listened calmly and then bent down to pick up another starfish and threw it into the sea. "It made a difference to that one."

And now I'd like to introduce you to a man who has inspired me to lead with love. Larry Broughton is a best-selling author, one of the top keynote leadership speakers in the country, and a former Green Beret. I chose Larry to be my special guest author for the "Leap with Love" chapter because every time I hear him speak, watch him interact with others, or have a personal conversation with him, I walk away feeling inspired to leap higher and love more.

Larry Broughton

> *Of all the possible habits, skills, strengths, and strategies you can apply to become a world-changer, if you don't include this one, I assure you that you're going to end up feeling hollow, empty, and unfulfilled.*

Many people go to their graves never fully understanding the most powerful and important high-impact habit and its effect on their professional careers and political pursuits, their personal lives and relationships, their academic and athletic achievements, and their spirits. When we embrace and engage in this habit, the world opens up to us, our spines are stiffened, we're brought to tears, and our horizons are expanded beyond anything that we've ever experienced. It all comes down to this: approach *all* things from a spirit of *love*.

I didn't understand this for most of my life either, so bear with me for a second. Don't tune out just yet. I know this might feel a little bit airy-fairy and a little squishy to you, but this is going to bring so many rewards to you and your life that people are going to be attracted to you like a magnet. They're going to support you, and they're going to help drive you toward the success and life of significance that you're seeking.

Although I've had my share of "success" throughout my life in the areas of athletics, military achievement, and entrepreneurial endeavors, my most significant heartache came from the breakdown and ultimate breakup of my marriage. It was on my road to recovery that I recognized that every "achievement" and every "failure" I'd experienced to that point was driven by the dark, divisive feeling of *fear*. I was afraid of lots of things back then: I was afraid that if people really knew me, they wouldn't like me. I was afraid that people would find out that I really didn't have any athletic talent at all, but only sheer drive that brought about my small victories. I was afraid that people would learn I was in over my head in my business dealings and then wouldn't respect me. And I was afraid of getting close to anyone, because I knew by doing so, I would have to share my most inner secrets and shame.

The truth is, fear had become a pretty heavy burden to carry around after all those years. I finally recognized that fear hijacks more dreams than failure ever will . . . but the good news, according to the New Testament's book of John, is that "perfect love drives out fear." Something powerful happens in the universe when we put our own agenda and fear aside for a moment and simply help someone else with a spirit of love. Something shifts in our soul when we lovingly serve others . . . we begin to look at ourselves differently and more lovingly. When we look at ourselves differently, we look at the world differently. There's something powerfully intimate about acts of loving service when we're not expecting anything in return.

Exercising a habit of love doesn't mean we become wimps. In fact, the most dangerous warriors I know have a loving spirit of compassion and service. The great news about loving and serving others is that you don't have to reenlist in the military or stop wearing designer clothes or stop drinking your favorite expensive coffee drinks. I'm not expecting you to sell your belongings and move to India to work with the poor. Lovingly serving others is really quite easy.

If you've never done something for someone else expecting nothing in return, then I encourage you to do so within the next twenty-four hours. You must take that first step.

How to Begin Serving Others
What I'm suggesting is that the next time you pull up to the grocery store or you're boarding a plane and you see someone struggling with their bags, help them out. When you see someone approaching the elevator, hold

the door open for them. When it's a busy day on the freeway, and you see someone frantically trying to cut into traffic, let them in and lovingly bless them rather than fighting for those few inches on the road. I'm asking you to give a pint of blood once in a while. I'm asking you to tutor a child who is struggling with their math homework.

I'm asking you to just do small things (with love), because I'll guarantee you this: if you've never given your time and heart expecting nothing in return, you're missing out on one of the most significant levels of joy and intimacy that you'll ever experience in life.

I can hear some of you asking, "Okay Larry, what does all this have to do with me becoming a better leader or helping me reach my own success goals?" Well, whether you've listened or not, you've likely heard it over and over again: no one reaches significant or sustainable success by themselves; it just doesn't happen. When you serve other people, the universe rewards you and the world opens up to you. People are attracted to you, and they want to help you reach your own goals.

So what do you have to do? **You have to take rapid action**. You can't sit around and dream of some big plan to change the world. You can't contemplate flowery ideas and hope that someday they're going to come to fruition, because it's simply not going to happen. You've got to take small, consistent (and loving) action steps.

I challenge you to seven days of loving service. Do one small act of service for someone else for seven days straight, and see what happens in your own life. Keep it simple, start small, and smile a lot.

Here's to your success. Now go do something significant today . . . go get 'em!

Daily Habit Action Steps

• What can you do today to leap with love?

• What could you do to make a difference in one person's life today?

• What could you do to start a chain reaction of kindness today in your community?

• Think of someone you know who may need some extra love in their life today, and write them a simple note of encouragement.

• Remember that you need not know a person to show them love. A simple thank-you to folks working in the grocery store, a kind smile as you pass someone on the street, letting someone in front of you on the freeway . . . What are some other things you could do for a stranger today?

• What if the news was all about spreading stories of love instead of fear? What kinds of stories could you share on the nightly news?

About the song "Take a Leap of Love"
After attending a leadership event with Larry Broughton and Craig Duswalt in Los Angeles in 2016, I couldn't wait to get back to my hotel room on the final night. I wanted to gather my notes from our two days together and put together a song that captured the essence of our time together. "Take a Leap of Love" is what came to me that night.

Take a Leap of Love
Inspired by Larry Broughton & Craig Duswalt
Music & Lyrics by Janie Lidey & Matt Wilder, BMI
©2016

It's who you are not what you are lean into your gift
Always lead with kindness this is
the life you came here to live
Decide to be the miracle in someone else's day
It's time to make the magic happen
in the Disney kind of way

Let your voice be heard let your hands reach out
Fill someone with hope 'cause
hope is what it's all about
Shine your brightest light and you will rise above
Give all you can give take the leap of love

It's who you are not what you are
that's where it all begins
You put your wheels in motion
And the journey never ends
Decide to be the miracle in someone else's day
It's time to make the magic happen
in the Disney kind of way

Let your voice be heard let your hands reach out
Fill someone with hope 'cause
hope is what it's all about
Shine your brightest light and you will rise above
Give all you can give take the leap of love
Take a leap of love—take a leap
of love—take the leap . . .

Let your voice be heard let your hands reach out
Fill someone with hope 'cause
hope is what it's all about
Shine your brightest light and you will rise above
Take a leap of love—take a leap of love—take a leap
The leap of love

Afterword

I believe that when you *act as if*, you will lean into your gift like never before and experience your wildest dreams. I believe that when you *begin it now*, doors will swing open wide for you, and a myriad of wonderful things will come your way. I believe that when you *dream big*, you will create an energy that will help allow blessings and miracles to appear in your life. I believe that when you *just imagine*, your thoughts will create your reality. I believe that the more you *live in gratitude*, the more things you will have to be grateful for. I believe that when you *let the music lift you*, you will feel like singing, even on the days when there is no song in your heart. I believe that when you *laugh while you leap*, you will find a greater sense of ease on your journey. And I believe that when you *leap with love*, you will carve the most direct path to your own peace, love, and happiness.

May you listen carefully to the song in your heart.
May you expect blessings and miracles along the way.
May your fears be calmed.
May you lean into your gift and find your North Star.
May you leap with faith!

About the Song "North Star"

After reading author and life coach Martha Beck's daily blogs and following her message through some of her other writings, it suddenly dawned on me that what she was talking about related on so many levels to how I was living my life. One day, in the midst of my meditation, "North Star" came to life.

North Star
Inspired by Martha Beck
Music & Lyrics by Janie Lidey, BMI
©2015

Today I asked the universe . . .

Teach me what I cannot see
Give me faith so that I can believe
Help me find the rhythm of my
soul and let her breathe
Turn on my light and let her shine
Help me dig a little deeper inside
And find the glow that I can leave behind

It's time to find your own North Star
Be still and let it form within your heart
It's a wild new world where you can
claim who you really are
Finding your own North Star

Quiet your mind from all the noise
Speak your truth and use your own voice
Put your faith in miracles and rejoice
Imagine like you were a little girl

Leap of Faith

Take the magic from the flicker of
a thought and let it whirl
Let your quiet power change the world

It's time to find your own North Star
Be still and let it form within your heart
It's a wild new world where you can
claim who you really are
Finding your own North Star

It's time to find your own North Star
Be still and let it form within your heart
It's a wild new world where you can
claim who you really are
Finding your own North Star
Finding your own North Star
Finding your own North Star

CD Info for the Music in *Leap of Faith*

Go to janielidey.com for information
on ordering your CD.

Each chapter in *Leap of Faith* ends with an original song that connects to the message in the story. Music has a way of raising our vibration and lifting us higher. It is my hope that these songs will give you an additional boost in powering up your leap. You can listen to samples of the songs on my website and then either order your CD directly from janielidey.com or find me on iTunes, CD Baby, and more . . .

I would like to thank the musicians that contributed to the production of this CD. They have all helped me rise to a higher standard in my journey as a musician, and beyond their remarkable musical talents, they are some of the kindest, most compassionate human beings on the planet. Their presence on this project is one of my big blessings and miracles.

Matt Wilder—Producer
Joey Turner—Additional Engineering
Mike Brignardello, Joeie Canaday & Gary Lunn—Bass
Perry Coleman, Jana Stanfield & Matt Wilder—
    Backup Vocals
Jenee Fleenor—Fiddle, Guitar, Mandolin and Backup
    Vocals

Buddy Hyatt, Jimmy Nichols & Matt Wilder—
Keyboards

Jerry Kimbrough & Matt Wilder—Acoustic & Electric
Guitar

Janie Lidey—Lead Vocals, Backup Vocals & Acoustic
Guitar

Russ Paul—Slide Guitar

Lonnie Wilson—Drums

About the Author

Janie Lidey is a speaker, author, singer, and Emmy-winning composer who dedicated herself to teaching music in the public schools of Alaska for twenty-six years. She started out teaching music in remote, fly-in-only villages, and in 2011, after seventeen years as the choir director and guitar teacher at Grammy Award–winning East High School, Janie stepped out of the safety and comfort of one school to make the world her classroom.

Lidey has been recognized for her excellence through winning an Emmy for her songwriting; a Grammy for the fine arts program she helped direct at East High School in Anchorage, Alaska; the Mayor's Arts Award, which recognizes excellence in music education; and a spot on the George Lucas Edutopia website for her role in helping make the world a better place. Mrs. Lidey not only taught her students to sing and play the guitar, she taught them to live their lives with passion, kindness, love, hope, and gratitude. The most important lesson was to instill the belief in her students that they could be or do anything they dreamed or imagined. Seeing the effect she was having on her students throughout the years made Janie feel a responsibility to step out and contribute on a global level.

Janie speaks to audiences across the country, inspiring them to take a leap of faith and create the life they have only dared to dream about. She has spoken at events including the Women Who Rock event in Los Angeles, California; the Rachel's Challenge Summit in Denver, Colorado; women's conferences in Alaska, California, and Iowa; the Lions Clubs International "8 to Great" event in Anchorage, Alaska; Relay for Life events along the West Coast; and personal growth events, to name a few. She also had the opportunity to perform alongside John Carter Cash at Willie Nelson's eightieth birthday tribute in Nashville, Tennessee.

Janie has lived in Alaska for over thirty years and has enjoyed many leaps of faith along the way. She taught music in eight remote, fly-in-only villages; was a forklift operator for a salmon fishery in Bristol Bay (where she occasionally sang and played her guitar in the saloon during fish closures); skied double black diamond, expert-only ski runs; paraglided off Hatcher Pass; ran a Segway tour business around Lake Hood; and built her own log home with her husband, Sean, where they have lived together with their son, Tristan, for fifteen years. They share their yard with an occasional mama and baby moose, black bear, brown bear, and lynx, but their favorite four-legged friend is their big yellow lab, Beaver.

www.janielidey.com

CPSIA information can be obtained
at www.ICGtesting.com
Printed in the USA
FSOW02n0407031016
25635FS